"Through the simple stories and practical principles in *Devotions for the Hungry Heart,* Shellie Rushing Tomlinson invites all comers to share her love for God and His Word. This little book could very well change your world, one day at a time."

–Pat Williams, Orlando Magic Senior Vice President and
author of *Coach Wooden's Forgotten Teams*

"If you're craving more of Jesus—the kind of feast that promises to make a heart full— *Devotions for the Hungry Heart* is like a beautifully laid table. I know few people who spark my hunger for my Savior as much as my friend Shellie does. Pull up a chair, friend, and dig in."

–Michele Cushatt, author of *I Am: A 60-day Journey
To Knowing Who You Are Because of Who He Is*

"From the moment I met Shellie, her love for Jesus emanated from her. In *Devotions for the Hungry Heart,* Shellie shares heartwarming stories that reveal that love and allow the reader to feel deeply and pursue passionately their own abiding love for Christ. Your hunger will be satiated and your soul will be filled!"

–Tracey Lanter Eyster, founder MomLifeToday.com,
author of *Be The Mom* and LifeWay's *Beautiful Mess Bible Study*

"As a friend, wife, mother, and human being on this earth, Shellie is one who loves in generous amounts. Her heart to serve us with truth, laughter, and some of the best food from the Creole State leaps off the pages of this book. As one who has the honor of knowing Shellie as friend, I champion this great offering with deep joy. After reading this book, I am confident you too will feel a kindred spirit in Shellie. Mostly, you will know the full and generous love of Jesus. With each daily devotion, His affection for you will satisfy the starved places of your mind, body, and soul. I highly recommend you carve out space in your day for this read. And then, carve a slice of Shellie's Layered Strawberry Pecan Delight. Both are heaven. Love you to the bones, Shellie. Thank you for this gift."

–Kasey Van Norman, bestselling author of *Named by God* and *Raw Faith*

"Shellie has a gift for making All Things Sacred super simple to understand. *Devotions for the Hungry Heart* serves up daily bread while whetting a healthy appetite for what truly matters in life. Some people push souls away with their inapproachable Christianese. Shellie slices through the heart and head like an ice cream headache. It hurts so good! I hope she has another book underway, because I'm already hungry for another helping."

–Nicole Seitz, author of *The Cage-maker* and *Trouble the Water*

"The hardest part of reading this devotional is sticking to one day. The temptation is to read ahead and devour the incredible, real life stories Shellie uses to illuminate scripture in her endearing belle style. During my next backyard He & Me Retreat, how will I ever not peek around for marauding redheaded cows during prayer time? Not only are the recipes totally yum, *Devotions for the Hungry Heart* serves up juicy, tasty, bite-sized morsels of the Bread of Life to satisfy the hungriest and thirstiest spirit. Another helping, please."

–Debora M. Coty, popular speaker, inspirational humorist and award-winning author
of 30 books, including the bestselling Too Blessed to be Stressed series

"In *Devotions for the Hungry Heart*, my friend Shellie is both witty and wise, timely and thought-provoking, southern and soul-searching. Whether our walk with Jesus is decades old or days old, these devotionals will create in each one of us a heart hungry for more of Jesus."

–Denise Hildreth Jones, author of *Reclaiming Your Heart*
founder and president of Reclaiming Hearts Ministries

"*Devotions for the Hungry Heart* is a delightful, engaging twenty-week adventure of digging into God's Word for refreshment, encouragement, and spiritual nourishment! Shellie Tomlinson has written a devotional that's filled with laugh-out-loud humor, poignant stories, and spot-on biblical truth. And don't miss the bonus of her favorite recipes!"

–Carol Kent, speaker and author

"Shellie has a way with comfort; whether it's a chat on her front porch, a slice of her farmhouse cake, or a well-timed encouragement from God's word, she's the one you go to when you need to be pointed in the right direction. In *Devotions for the Hungry Heart*, you're getting the best of everything Shellie has to offer between two covers: her wisdom, her humor, and a food-sensibility that can only be found south of the Mason Dixon line. This California girl was transported not just to Shellie's kitchen for the feast, but to her kitchen table for the deep conversation."

–Kathi Lipp, bestselling writer and author of *Clutter Free* and *Overwhelmed*

"The first time I sat down with this book, my plan was to read just the devotional for the day. I read ten. What a pleasure! Spending time in the pages of one of Shellie's books is like lingering over coffee with a funny, insightful friend. Best of all, this gifted writer uses her engaging stories to draw readers effortlessly toward Jesus. Shellie doesn't begin with any assumptions about the spiritual condition of her readers—she engages you wherever you are and nudges you forward with humor and grace. Without a doubt, this delightful read will leave you hungrier—and more satisfied—than when you began."

–Karen Linamen Bouchard, speaker and author of *Just Hand Over the Chocolate and No One Will Get Hurt* and a dozen other books for women

"Shellie has written a candid devotional full of life stories that will make you laugh one minute and cry the next. Her personal narratives consistently point us back to Jesus, as we seek to make God famous. Perfect bite-sized morsels of truth for the busy woman make you long for the next day's reading, if you can have the self-control to wait until then! Equally delicious are the recipes—stick to your ribs dishes and lighter ones too! You'll be so glad you picked up these pages of God's truth for you. I know His words, through Shellie, will feed your hungry heart as it did mine."

–Lisa Lloyd, speaker, actor, and author of *Chasing Famous: Living the Life You've Always Auditioned For*

Chasing Jesus Six Days from Sunday

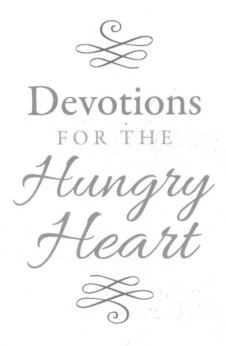

Devotions
FOR THE
Hungry
Heart

Shellie Rushing Tomlinson

SHILOH RUN PRESS
An Imprint of Barbour Publishing, Inc.

Introduction

Hey, y'all! I'm beyond excited about sharing these devotions together. You, my friend, have heaven's full attention. Yes, you. Lean in and I'll explain.

Devotions for the Hungry Heart is built on God's promises that He will be found by the seeker and satisfy those who hunger for Him. This is why I can say with confidence that simply being drawn to this book is positioning you for more of the fulfilling Christian experience you may have heard of or read about. You know, the one you think is beyond your reach, but the one God offers each of us through Jesus, His Son and our Savior.

But perhaps you're thinking, *I don't think you understand, Shellie. What if I'm not quite sure why I picked up this book? What if the truth is that I'm not that hungry for God? Do you have anything for someone like me?*

You better believe it. I have a boatload of personal experience for you. I've been where you are. I've been the believer who wondered how it was that some people could be so passionate and hungry for God when the most I could muster for Him was a healthy respect. I know what it's like to be secretly ashamed of my lukewarm faith, to wonder if I could ever be one of those desperate-for-more-of-Jesus people—and I know what it's like to have a growing passion for the Son of God that is stronger than I ever could have imagined. In short, I know what it's like to hunger to be spiritually hungry, and I know what it's like to develop a growing and ravenous desire for God's company.

Whether you have a healthy craving for more of Jesus or the barely discernible taste for a relationship with Him that seems beyond your reach, the glorious truth is that God put that hunger in your heart in the first place; and God is more willing to fan that flame, than you or I ever could be, to see it combust. I'm excited about coming alongside you and sharing six traits that I've discovered over the years that stir my appetite for a God-sized feast. Oh, and bonus time: I'll meet you in the middle of these pages with some of my favorite recipes to fill your physical tummy. Truly, if this book came with a dinner bell, I'd be ringing it like crazy right about now. Come on, y'all. The table is set and dinner is served. Let's eat!

"Ho! Every one who thirsts, come to the waters;
and you who have no money come, buy and eat. Come,
buy wine and milk without money and without cost."

ISAIAH 55:1

*We'll be unchanging or
ever growing, and it will all
hinge on whether we live
with a surrendered will.*

A Hungry Heart Is Surrendered

I ran across a fascinating story about the late newspaper publisher William Randolph Hearst. I want to share it with you because of the tremendous truth it holds.

As the story goes, the extremely wealthy Mr. Hearst was an avid art collector who spared no expense in acquiring costly artifacts from all over the world. One day, after reading about some exceedingly rare items, Mr. Hearst decided he simply had to have them in his possession. So he sent an assistant around the world in search of them. Mr. Hearst was determined to discover who owned these items and how much it would cost him to acquire them. Finally, after months of searching abroad, Mr. Hearst's employee reported that the treasure had been found—in a warehouse belonging to Mr. Hearst. Yes, Mr. Hearst had been willing to pay whatever cost was involved for treasure he already owned. If only he had scanned the inventory list of his own blessings.

Friends, I believe that's a picture of us as believers, especially the American church, which has been so well fed on God's Word. We're constantly looking for that extra something, that latest devotional, the newest translation, when everything we really need to live a fruitful Christian life lies within us. We are rich in Christ Jesus! We have all we need to partner with God in the sanctification process through Jesus, Immanuel, the hope of glory. (Don't panic at the word *sanctification*. Just think of it as being transformed through growth.)

How will we do this? How will we partner with God to see the manifestation of the gift of Christ within us? The Word teaches that our lives rise or fall on our individual wills. We'll be ineffective, so-so saints, never changing, never growing—or we'll be constantly in the process of being transformed, being made new, and exploring the riches that are ours in Christ Jesus. And this will hinge on whether we live with our wills surrendered to God.

> *"Truly, truly, I say to you,*
> *unless a grain of wheat falls into*
> *the earth and dies, it remains alone;*
> *but if it dies, it bears much fruit."*
>
> JOHN 12:24

A Hungry Heart Is Intentional

I dropped the big juvenile bottle of bubble bath in my cart with a grin on my lips and the old jingle playing in my head, *"Mr. Bubble in the tub'll get you squeaky clean. . . ."* The soap was an impulse buy, but oh, it was worth it. That evening I enjoyed a trip down memory lane and a mini vacation all rolled up in one brimming bathtub, compliments of Mr. Bubble.

A sudsy bath with Mr. Bubble ranks right up there on my list of favorite childhood memories. We didn't enjoy the experience on a regular basis either. This wasn't an oversight. Mr. Bubble was a luxury in our penny-pinching world, but when he did make an appearance, our regular bath times paled in comparison. And, trust me here, he outpaced Mama's infamous spit baths by a country mile and then some. My sisters and I weren't expected to participate much in Mama's spit baths. We were simply expected to sit still and endure the washing as she wet her finger and cleaned our faces. The end result—we got clean, clean enough to be seen in public, anyway.

I see an analogy here that's worth digging out and holding up to the light. Scripture teaches that the Word of God washes us from our sins. We receive both an initial rebirth and a continual cleansing. And yet one of the greatest tragedies the church as a body struggles under is our willingness to settle with spiritual spit baths from those in authority.

Am I thankful we can hear God's Word through others? Absolutely. I'm extremely grateful for the many fine teachers and preachers I've learned from, but I have a message I'd like to take to the ends of this world. Being content to hear His Word second-hand rather than personally and purposefully soaking ourselves in the Word's deep waters on our own time is like settling for a spit bath over a tub of Mr. Bubble. There's simply no comparison.

> *They received the word with great eagerness,*
> *examining the Scriptures daily to see*
> *whether these things were so.*
> ACTS 17:11

A Hungry Heart Is Praying

I was minding my own business and typing away on my laptop when I noticed something out of my peripheral vision. Something large was moving across my backyard. I turned around to discover a redheaded cow loitering on my property. *Surprise!* It was bizarre—the redhead and her cow suit.

If you knew my BFF, you would be ahead of me at this point. Yes, it was Rhonda (also known to my readers and radio listeners as Red), and she was strolling across my backyard wearing a cow outfit and acting for all the world like it was the most normal thing a middle-aged woman could be doing on a beautiful fall day. I grabbed my phone and documented the moment with video footage and a weak joke about how "utterly" ridiculous she looked. I love corny puns.

To be fair, why Red had a cow outfit in her possession isn't that strange, even if meandering through my backyard in said costume was, but I'll need to skip the backstory to move this along. Bottom line—Red knew we'd both get a chuckle out of it, and we do so enjoy a good laugh. There's also the maturity thing. Red and I haven't grown up. Nor do we plan to anytime soon, which brings me to a more serious takeaway from the cow moment.

It's okay to be young at heart; but as believers, you and I are supposed to be growing up, and it should be obvious to all that we are maturing in our love for God and each other.

As a follower of Christ, I shouldn't be the same person day in, day out, year in, year out, stagnant in spirit and devoid of growth, and neither should you. Growth isn't about bearing down and forcing maturity, however. That fails every time. Just spend time talking with Jesus, y'all. He's like Miracle-Gro. You'll be transformed and ever growing, and the first person surprised by the change will be the one doing the changing.

Speaking the truth in love,
we are to grow up in every way into
him who is the head, into Christ.
EPHESIANS 4:15 ESV

THURSDAY

A Hungry Heart Is Celebrating

I see hearts all around me. I've seen them in big puffy, white clouds, and I've seen them in the knots of old oak trees. I've seen them drawn into the scales of a fish and outlined on the back of an insect. I can trace this fascination to the earliest days of writing a book called *Heart Wide Open*, and I've never gotten over it, and I'm okay with that. I hope I never do.

I once mentioned this heart thing to my oldest grandson. He was six at the time. We were walking across a parking lot holding hands when I pulled him to a stop and showed him a heart formed from the mortar of the pavement at our feet. "God shows me those," I told Grant. "He knows I like to see them, so He shows them to me. It's like a little note from heaven right in the middle of the day. When I see it, I think about how much God loves us, and I have a little party in my own heart."

My next trip to Houston to see the "Grand Boys of Texas" featured a sweet surprise. I learned that Grant Thomas had become a heart seeker in his own right. And he was good at it! Grant showed me all kinds of hearts around his house, and his mommy said he'd been showing her hearts all around Humble. Of course, the hearts have been there all the time. Grant is just now seeing them because he's just now looking for them and expecting to find them.

While I am unapologetically guilty when it comes to over-sharing grandchildren stories, I offer this tale to share a deeper truth I've discovered about pursuing God. If we walk in this world demanding special visions or revelations from God that He might prove His existence to us, we seldom find the evidence of God we're after. However, if we abandon such egocentric demands and focus instead on looking for God and celebrating Him in our unspectacular everyday lives, we find that He is all around us and He has been here all the time.

> *"[God] made from one man every nation*
> *of mankind. . .that they would seek God, if perhaps*
> *they might grope for Him and find Him, though He is*
> *not far from each one of us; for in Him we live and*
> *move and exist, as even some of your own poets*
> *have said, 'For we also are His children.'"*
>
> ACTS 17:26–28

A Hungry Heart Is Needy

A light fog blanketing the landscape can be calming to the soul. For instance, sitting on my back porch talking to the good Lord while the early morning is trying to slip out of its thin, pale robe is a nice prescription for peace.

There are other times when fog is less appreciated, like when you're driving. Or how about when a cloud begins to roll up from the floorboards of an airplane cabin as you're flying through the friendly skies with a group of polite strangers? That's not so relaxing. But it's exactly where I found myself a couple of years back.

I remember how uncomfortable my fellow travelers and I were at the onset of the mist, and I remember how our pilot's cheerful announcement over the PA did little to alleviate our growing apprehension, not when he told us it was "nothing to be concerned about," and not when he explained the small "incidental wiring issue" behind it. We were eager to chill, just as soon as we got our feet on the ground. In the end, the fog of smoke dissipated as slowly as it had arrived, and we landed without incident.

"Don't worry, be happy" may have been good advice that day, but you and I would be unwise to adopt it as a blanket prescription against all early warning signs; and we'd be especially foolhardy to ignore the internal God-given monitor of our conscience. For the snare that trips us up in the walk of faith is rarely the obvious one.

Sin is stealthy, and apathy—why, apathy rolls in as silently and insidiously as fog. Our inner warning system might go off when we first start choosing other activities over church or when we quit praying quite as often and open our Bibles even less. But the alert grows fainter over time, and the less attention we pay to the growing fog of apathy, the more it builds until we can't see the forest for the trees and we can't find the way back home to Jesus if our lives depended on it. And they do.

But each one is tempted when he is carried
away and enticed by his own lust. Then when
lust has conceived, it gives birth to sin; and when
sin is accomplished, it brings forth death.

JAMES 1:14–15

A Hungry Heart Is Sharing

I once enjoyed an invigorating worship session in my backyard that I'm sure gave my neighbors cause to lock their doors. Backstory? I like to rework and redeem secular songs, offering them up to God with an entirely new twist from the intentions of the one who penned them. I don't know what the Righteous Brothers would've thought of my version to their hit song "You've Lost That Lovin' Feeling," but I've crooned about my commitment to get down on my knees for my One and Only for years now. Go ahead. Laugh. But I think He loves it.

On the specific morning that comes to mind, I pulled a similar switcheroo on the late Percy Sledge. For the record (weak pun intended), the lyrics to "Cover Me" make a beautiful praise song when sung to Jesus. Indeed, I do want Him to spread His precious love all over this needy belle. And yes, I performed that selection that day with my tennis racket as a stand-in guitar. Right there in the backyard in front of God and everybody.

The racket was a handy replacement for a musical instrument I had begun using to try and tire Dixie Belle, my late chocolate Lab, during what she preferred to be an endless game of fetch. You should be grateful to get this story in print. It spares you an audio encore. But enough of my less-than-captivating entertainment career; I want to make a deeper point about my secular/sacred music session.

I speak at all sorts of events, many of them Christian, some of them civic, or what might be deemed secular. My aim is to respect the wishes of the event planner. If I'm there for entertainment, I'll give you laughs. If you want Jesus, I'm your girl. Both? Oh, I'm all in!

I once enjoyed the "sacred" events more than the secular ones, but not anymore. I've become convinced of the importance of being fully present in every moment of our believing lives. If we pour ourselves wholeheartedly into a Christian event but we don't engage with others at work, for example, we effectively divide and therefore diminish the light that's in us. The Bible says our gospel light is for the highest hill, not the underside of a basket. You don't have to play air guitar or wear a clown outfit, but if you're a believer, you are called to shine. Whatever that looks like on you, shine on.

"Let your light shine before men in
such a way that they may see your good works,
and glorify your Father who is in heaven."
Matthew 5:16

A Hungry Heart Is Surrendered

We have a lovely lakeside walking trail here in my hometown. I particularly enjoy walking it in the late evenings, as the natural light of day is closing and the ornamental streetlamps begin to glow. Not long ago, I was walking along this path when the message of a small sign posted beside the trail arrested my thoughts, WALK AT YOUR OWN RISK.

I knew the purpose behind the sign was to ward off potential personal injury claims, but as the caution began looping in my mind, my thoughts turned to their application for our Christian walk.

I took a picture of the sign that day to remind myself, and anyone else who chooses to listen, that to follow Christ is not merely to risk our lives; it is to lose them. So I've been thinking: perhaps we should add a similar caution to our church signs. Something like, "FOLLOW JESUS AT YOUR OWN RISK. DETAILS INSIDE." You might say, "But Shellie, that kind of message isn't exactly a big draw." I would agree, at least not to those interested in adding Jesus to their lives instead of surrendering all they are to all He is.

On the other hand, those who truly laid down their lives at the foot of the cross would actually find them! And that means our churches wouldn't be full of people saddle sore from riding the fence and road weary from wondering why their Christian experience falls so short of what the church has advertised, when walking through life with Jesus Christ is anything but boring.

When we die daily to walk with the God-man, we soon discover that His presence is worth every single step. How's that for a sign worth posting?

> *"Whoever wishes to save his life will lose it;*
> *but whoever loses his life for My sake will find it."*
> MATTHEW 16:25

A Hungry Heart Is Intentional

"Shellie Coon, I hate to bother you."

"You're not bothering me, Papa. What's up?"

The use of my childhood name, combined with the reluctance I heard in Papa's voice, told me it was serious. It was. Papa had computer problems. I'm no computer expert, but you'll never convince Papa of that. He thinks I'm Billie Ruth Gates. As Papa began describing the funny things his computer was doing, I couldn't help wondering if it had anything to do with the night I called to warn him about the Conficker worm.

"I'm sorry for calling so late," I told him that fateful night, "but you need to turn your computer off until I can figure out how to protect us from the Conficker worm." My man and I had laughed ourselves silly at Papa's response. "Well, baby," Papa said, "your mama and I are in bed, and I'm not getting back up. That worm will just have to eat its way through the blame thing."

We were still chuckling when Papa continued, "Besides, I'm thinking my problem has something to do with that McGruffie." It may sound like Papa had jumped to McGruff the Crime Dog, but knowing Papa, I knew he was referring to his security software.

"Is it up to date?" I asked.

"What's that?"

"Your antivirus program—"

"Well now, I don't know...."

The short of this story is that Papa's issues were so serious his PC had to go to the computer hospital, and that sets us up for an important takeaway. As believers, we have an enemy who is always trying to breach our defenses. The bad news is that the devil will bombard us with as much fear and negativity as we're willing to absorb. The good news is that we've been given the Word of God to protect us from his attacks. God's Word can identify and deal with these threats to your peace of mind immediately. However, just like Papa's antivirus program, the Word in us needs to be intentionally installed with regular updates. So, tell me, are you protected?

Every word of God is tested;
He is a shield to those who take refuge in Him.

PROVERBS 30:5

Welcoming God into our world
first thing in the morning
positions us to live in His
soul-restoring presence all day.

❧ WEDNESDAY ❧

A Hungry Heart Is Praying

Awhile back I made an admission to my radio listeners and website subscribers. I understand it came as a surprise to some who were convinced that I must jump out of bed every morning like Tigger the boisterous tiger. The reality is that I wake up with an outlook closer to Eeyore the dismal donkey. Oh, I morph into Tigger, all right, but I start out as Eeyore, and I have for a long time. Let me explain.

My first conscious thoughts every single morning of my life are irrationally gloomy and colored with familiar feelings of hopelessness that suggest living is more drudgery than delight—and really, why bother? This has been going on for years, and I can rarely trace it to anything concrete that's going on in my life.

For the longest time, I begged the Lord to take this weighty thing away from me. It persisted. I've since quit asking. I still don't understand it, but I trust He has reasons for allowing it. I've learned instead to take the ugly to Him faster than quick. I now begin my days by slipping out of bed to my knees. This is not my daily prayer time. As a matter of fact, I'm only there briefly, mere seconds, but they are life-changing moments. From something that once felt like a curse has come the sweetest of blessings as I invite God into my world from the get-go.

I have an old song on my laptop called "Welcome to My World." It reminds me of the invitation God makes to each of us to share our lives with Him. Google it. (Go ahead. I'll wait.) Close your eyes and listen to the lyrics; try to hear them as a message from the Lover of your soul.

Beautiful, yes? I've discovered the great joy of accepting God's offer and welcoming Him right back into my world. If you haven't discovered His soul-restoring solace, there's simply no time like the present!

O satisfy us in the morning with Your lovingkindness,
that we may sing for joy and be glad all our days.
PSALM 90:14

THURSDAY

A Hungry Heart Is Celebrating

Years ago I found myself in the middle of a chicken-and-egg routine. I was trying to get a traditional publisher interested in my first little book. After filing dozens upon dozens of rejection slips away by date of dismissal, I realized I was in for a challenge. (I'm quick like that, and compulsive.) Determined to get up to speed, I started reading everything I could about the publishing world.

I learned some very interesting things. I discovered that people who are already published stand a greater chance of getting published than people who have never been published. I also learned that people who are represented by agents have a better chance of getting published than people without agents. Did I mention that agents like to represent people who have already been published? I felt like the punch line of a bad joke.

Fast-forward a couple years, I was trying to take my little "All Things Southern" party past the Internet and into the radio world. As Yogi would say, "It was déjà vu all over again."

"Shellie," I was told, "you'll need a good sponsor to get on a lot of radio stations." That sounded hard enough, but then they threw another egg at me! "Shellie, you'll need to be on a lot of radio stations to attract a good-sized sponsor." I don't mind telling you I was often tempted to fry the chicken and scramble the egg!

I've since seen some forward progress (and more than my share of backward motion, but that's another devotion). Can I just say that my chicken-and-egg experiences have left me eternally grateful that the Good Lord doesn't play that game! I'm so glad He doesn't say, "Clean yourselves up as best you can and then I'll be your Savior." I'd be washing and wiping without a hope. Nor does He say, "I'll be your Savior, but then you'll have to be perfect." I'd be doomed again! On the contrary, Romans 5:8 says that while we were sinners, Christ died for us. Jesus, the sinless substitute, exchanges our sins for His salvation, and then He teaches us how to live a victorious life. And, praise God, there's not a chicken or an egg in sight!

For if while we were enemies we were
reconciled to God through the death of His Son,
much more, having been reconciled,
we shall be saved by His life.
ROMANS 5:10

FRIDAY

A Hungry Heart Is Needy

I just downed a bottle of water in one long gulp. It surprised me when the plastic caved in on itself. I didn't realize I was so thirsty until I started guzzling. And that, of course, reminded me of a story.

Our son and daughter were gifted athletes. That's not an empty mama brag. The two of them excelled in a number of high school sports. Jessica and Phillip had a lot of similarities in how they approached competition, but also some distinct differences. Take tennis. Phillip gave himself every opportunity to perform well by paying attention to the fuel he was putting in his body before a match, and he made sure he had plenty of liquid with him for the duration of the competition. His sister? Please.

Despite my best and often repeated advice (Jessica might have said "nagging," but I'm telling this story), our daughter paid scant attention to her pregame nutrition. What's worse, Jessica had this thing where she wouldn't allow herself to drink water on changeovers if she wasn't playing like she thought she should. She literally punished herself while she tried to turn the tide.

Today Jessica and I can laugh at that memory together. Denying yourself what you need the most because you aren't performing well? Going without water until you're so thirsty you suck the bottom out of the bottle? Who does these things? All of us. But I'll take a public look in the mirror and allow y'all to learn from my experience.

I can be sorely thirsting for the presence of Jesus and let the cares of the day get in my way until I'm parched for His peace. That's sad. But let me tell you what's worse. I've also made poor decisions in the past about whether I can drink from His inexhaustible well based on my current judgment of my present performance. Even today when I know that's faulty reasoning, I'm apt to fall victim to such stinking thinking. That's equally tragic. Friends, Jesus is Living Water. We are desperate for Him, and He alone qualifies us to quench our thirsty souls.

On the last day, the climax of the festival,
Jesus stood and shouted to the crowds,
"Anyone who is thirsty may come to me!
Anyone who believes in me may come and drink!"
John 7:37–38 NLT

SATURDAY

A Hungry Heart Is Sharing

Last year my BFF celebrated my birthday in her delightfully un-orthodox style. Knowing I was meeting myself coming and going, she snuck over to my house at midnight with a slow cooker of roast and veggies and plugged it in on my back porch. And then she taped silly pictures to my plate glass doors and left cards and gifts. Cards and gifts are plural. Over the years Red and I have adopted a "more is more" approach to each other's birthdays. She even gifted me with Wonder Woman pj's. There's more to that story, but let's use the superhero thread as a call to action for all of us instead.

Did you know disciples of Christ are equipped with super-powers? It's true. We can choose to plug into otherworldly strength—or not. How about a story for illustration?

Take someone whose words cut as often as they encourage. It's difficult to respond to anyone who does that, but it's even harder if that person professes to be a believer. Do I speak the truth? Well, I have a theory. I think it's possible that this believer may be forgiven but not feel forgiven—and hence he or she can't live forgiving.

We tend to think such people don't feel remorse for their

spitefulness, but what if it's just the opposite? What if they live in a self-made, self-maintained prison, punishing themselves for the past? And what if the bars of that cage grow stronger every time they give in to bitterness and lash out because it gives them yet another reason to hate themselves more.

But wait. What if those same bars get weaker when our response to the ugliness of those people is more love and forgiveness? What if we're the factor that will determine if they bury themselves in self-hate or are eventually fully healed? What if all that depends on you and me choosing to act out of the new nature Christ gave us?

Jesus can do through us what we could never do in our own strength—if we'll respond to others out of real-time devotion to Him. Now go be a superhero. Somebody you know needs one.

Be kind to one another, tender-hearted,
forgiving each other, just as God in
Christ also has forgiven you.
EPHESIANS 4:32

MONDAY

A Hungry Heart Is Surrendered

"Strut over here and you'll be limping back." I was probably in junior high the first time I heard that zinger, but I didn't need anyone to translate it. I instinctively understood those were throw-down words, meant to inform the person who was brewing for a fight that the speaker was fully prepared to do battle.

I like to give credit where credit is due, but I've been unsuccessful in tracing that line to the original source. On the other hand, it's reminiscent of a certain Bible story, and I do know where that's found.

In Genesis 32 we read of a long-ago night when a patriarch of the faith named Jacob wrestled with an angel of God. The Bible later reveals that this mysterious man was God Himself. At the conclusion of their wrestling, just as dawn was breaking, God gave Jacob His blessing. And then God touched Jacob's hip in such a way that left the biblical figure with a distinctive limp that would serve as a lifetime reminder of what had transpired.

That narrative is dear to me these days because I walk with my own God-given limp. What's more, I never want it to heal.

God knew from the moment of my salvation that I would need continual cleansing and continual enabling by His Spirit to walk with Him. Sadly, it took me a lot longer to figure this out. Once saved, I set off in full confidence to do this Christian thing with the insurance slip of my conversion in my hip pocket. Only my life didn't look anything like the overcoming, abundant experience I saw detailed in His book. I didn't have to wrestle with God as long as I did to learn that I needed Him on an ongoing basis, and not just for my salvation. I live to help others figure that out more quickly than I did, but I'm forever thankful that it finally got through this thick head of mine. I now walk with a God-given limp that has me leaning heavily on my sweet Jesus. I know full well that I can't live for Him without living with Him. In other words, I may have strutted out, but I limped back—and our relationship is all the stronger for it. A forever limp is a wonderful thing. I hope you have one of your own.

> *"I am the vine, you are the branches;*
> *he who abides in Me and I in him,*
> *he bears much fruit, for apart from*
> *Me you can do nothing."*
> JOHN 15:5

TUESDAY

A Hungry Heart Is Intentional

"But it's all touching!" The woeful complaint came from my friend's son. Bless his heart. From where I sat, it looked like his mother had done a good job of segregating the food on Welton's plate, but I sympathized with the little fellow's distress. I never could make my parents understand that it was impossible to redeem my fast-food hamburger simply by removing a tomato slice—not when it had been contaminated from the juice and seeds of said tomato.

That was back in the day when my sisters and I considered a balanced meal to be equal helpings of meat and potatoes. And bread, we made exceptions for bread, especially Mama's cat-head biscuits or hot, buttered corn bread, but we were allergic to the idea of eating anything that didn't fall in these sanctioned categories.

These days I enjoy eating cabbage, broccoli, and a host of other things that come in shades of green. My tastes have changed over time, just as Mama said they would. I've often heard people use changing taste buds as an analogy for developing a desire for God's Word, claiming that the more of it we read, the more of it we'll want. I may even have used that line of thinking myself. I honestly don't remember; but if I did, I'd like to clarify that message.

Experience has taught me that a person can read the Bible for years without coming to love and hunger for its holy truth—if, that is, the reading is done out of compulsion. Why? Because unlike any other book, the Bible is alive. I don't believe God's Word opens to the person who reads it out of obligation. With a little persuasion, I could even be convinced that it actively resists the intellectual reader who studies it with no other goal than to try and disprove what she or he is reading. No, to fall in love with the Truth that is the Holy Scripture, you must come to it for life itself. Come to feast, my friend, and you'll be fed.

"The words that I speak to
you are spirit, and they are life."
JOHN 6:63 NKJV

WEDNESDAY

A Hungry Heart Is Praying

I've never made a secret of the fact that I couldn't talk well when I was young, and I've freely admitted that traces of my childhood speech impediment can still be heard today. (Some would say those disclosures are unnecessary. These would be the people who have heard me speak in person.)

I've also mentioned a time or two thousand that I once had a speech therapist who worked with me in elementary school who liked to hold on to my tongue while putting me through his little speech-improvement regimen. Why don't you read that again? I'll wait.

Gospel truth, y'all. The man would literally hold my tongue and ask me to repeat after him. Can you imagine? I remember thinking that I couldn't talk well when I had sole control of my tongue. What on earth made him think the two of us could get better results if he held on to it for me confounded mini-me. I do hope they've abandoned that practice.

Years later (because I am an eternal optimist), I signed up for high school Spanish. The results weren't much better. Don't bother asking me to roll an *r*. I couldn't do it then; can't do it to this day. I mean this in the nicest way, but if you want an *r* rolled, you'll need to roll it yourself.

My peers may not have had my particular challenge, but I don't remember Spanish coming that easy for them either. That's understandable. Experts tell us that young children have an easier time learning new languages. The older we are, the more challenging it is for us to learn new sentence structures and the harder it becomes for us to pronounce previously foreign sounds. It's not impossible, mind you, just difficult.

Many of the same things can be said about learning to pray. First Thessalonians 5:17 tells us to pray without ceasing. It sounds like a tall order when we first hear it. Our sentences sound all King James textbook-y and we find ourselves stuttering and stretching for the right words. That said, I beg you not to become discouraged and quit. I doubt Spanish will ever roll off this belle's tongue, but talking to God has become as easy as breathing in and breathing out, and you can know this same delight. Can you imagine?

I love the Lord, because He hears
my voice and my supplications.
Psalm 116:1

THURSDAY

A Hungry Heart Is Celebrating

What do you get when you bake chocolate muffins, top them with small mountains of peanut butter mousse frosting, and cool them in the fridge before dipping them upside down in melted hot chocolate that forms a hard shell over that melt-in-your-mouth icing? Answer: very happy All Things Southern grandchildren, wired for sound. I'm certain my daughter and daughter-in-law were ready to paint a bull's-eye on my back the day the littles and I whipped these up together, but the grands gave me high marks indeed. (And really, who do you think I was aiming to please?)

I remember sharing one of our delicacies with Grant Thomas, the oldest grandson. I could tell he enjoyed the first forkful, but then he got a bite with just the right proportions of muffin, mousse, and chocolate. Grant looked at me with those big, beautiful dark eyes dancing in his sweet face and whispered, "Keggie, I want to keep this bite in my mouth all day." I thought that was the best definition I've ever heard of what it means to savor something.

You know, it would be a waste of your time to tell me or Grant that those cupcakes weren't supersweet. We tasted them for ourselves! In much the same way, those who learn to savor God's truth for themselves develop a rock-solid appreciation of its goodness that can't be shaken regardless of any worldly arguments against it—and there's no downside.

Consuming sugar-laden chocolate–peanut butter muffins on a regular basis wouldn't be good for any of us, but God's words are a win-win. Oh, come, let us savor the sweet Word of God. It is satisfying today and rewarding tomorrow!

Eat honey, my son, for it is good, and the
honeycomb is sweet to your palate;
realize that wisdom is the same for you.
If you find it, you will have a future,
and your hope will never fade.
PROVERBS 24:13–14 HCSB

If we bear His name,
we should carry His likeness.

A Hungry Heart Is Needy

One day I plan to be a superorganized author like some of my friends. I watch these people like a calf staring at a new gate.

At the last book festival I attended, I packed an adorable little rolling cart with everything I'd need to try once more to be that person. Upon my arrival, I wheeled up to a massive set of double doors. On the other side, a large audience sat listening to a panel already in progress. At least they were listening before yours truly and her trusty cart started trying to get in those blasted doors. They weren't locked, but they did decide to be contrary just for me—so contrary that by the time I got one opened and stepped inside, everyone had turned to see who was making all the noise. And that's when, with all eyes on me, the wheel fell off my rolling cart, sending it crashing into the wall and spilling all my organized authory things. Yes, really.

"Wherever I go, there I am."

I've said that forever. I thought I made it up until recently when I heard it from other directions. Apparently I picked it up along the way. Several days after that lovely moment, I said it again. Only this time, I was thanking Jesus for His ongoing intercession in the lives of believers, telling Him how badly I need such a Savior.

"Because," I said, "wherever I go, there I am."

And that's when I felt His precious inside voice ask me to repeat that line. I did. *"Slower,"* I felt Him say, *"and just the last part."* This time when I repeated the words "There I am," I heard in them the famous name by which God identified Himself in the Old Testament. He is the great I AM. This is why it's so critical that we believers continually recognize how much we need Jesus and resort to Him. The Bible says we're transformed by beholding Him; and if we dare bear His name, we should carry His likeness.

For wherever I go, there I AM.

But we all, with unveiled face,
beholding as in a mirror the glory of the Lord,
are being transformed into the same
image from glory to glory.

2 CORINTHIANS 3:18

A Hungry Heart Is Sharing

He was small for his age, his voice timid. The clothes he wore hung in folds on his body. I wondered if whoever bought them had done so with growing room in mind. His glasses took up the upper half of his face. While his classmates grinned, laughed, and did their best to find something, anything with which to weigh in on my presentation, he seemed perfectly willing, even anxious, to blend into the background. Clearly, he was most comfortable in anonymity. And yet I can't seem to forget him.

The last time I saw him, he was standing in a classroom clutching a piece of paper bearing my autograph, as if having it gave him something of value. Believe me, I realize how silly that is. That slip of paper held nothing of worth. The value lay in the child holding it. In the role of visiting author at his school, I'd done my best to leave every child there with that message: "You matter. And it's not based on your performance or the status of your family. If you breathe in and out, you have purpose." I hope someone waters those words.

Life has always been hard, but I can't imagine being a kid today. The news offers murder rates and Hollywood updates in the same breath. Keep the teleprompter rolling; time is money.

Message given and received: kick a ball, write a song, or design a new computer program, but do it fast. Your value is in your production, and you're not going to live forever. Talk about pressure!

Society is paying a huge price for letting our children believe they just happened along. How valuable can life be when there is no Creator, no purpose—here today, gone tomorrow? Let's stop the nonsense. Let's tell children they were born for eternity and free them from the shadow of worldly expectations, or what the preacher of Ecclesiastes masterfully referred to as "vanity of vanities." There is only one shadow where all who come find passion and purpose, and that's the shadow of the cross.

For You formed my inward parts; You wove me in my mother's womb. I will give thanks to You, for I am fearfully and wonderfully made; wonderful are Your works, and my soul knows it very well. My frame was not hidden from You, when I was made in secret, and skillfully wrought in the depths of the earth; Your eyes have seen my unformed substance; and in Your book were all written the days that were ordained for me, when as yet there was not one of them. How precious also are Your thoughts to me, O God! How vast is the sum of them! If I should count them, they would outnumber the sand. When I awake, I am still with You.

PSALM 139:13–18

A Hungry Heart Is Surrendered

Years ago, I wrote about a graveyard game I once played with my cousins, and I included it in my first book, *Lessons Learned on Bull Run Road*. Odds are you haven't read that little book, so allow me to recap that story. Many nights when the adults were inside sharing stories, we cousins would slip next door to the church where our Papaw Stone preached fire and brimstone, and the games would begin.

One such game required participants to venture as far into the pitch-black graveyard that adjoined the churchyard as nerves would allow and touch the farthest tombstone a sojourner could reach before trembling legs turned on their owners and propelled them back to safety. Security beckoned in the form of a single lightbulb that hung over the front steps of Riverside Baptist Church, and even now I remember running for that glow as if my life depended on it while trying my hardest not to step on the graves in my path.

We had been taught, rightfully so, to respect the burial places of those laid to rest. I wanted to honor that idea, but I also wanted to outrun the booger bears I felt sure were gaining on me. It's with a similar respect that I make the following confession.

I am discovering where true life is found, and it has me jumping on my grave.

Not my literal grave, of course. I'm talking about learning something of what the great apostle Paul knew, that the joy and the strength of a life lived in Christ Jesus is found in dying daily, in surrendering my right to me—and doing it over and over again. I don't have this thing down by any stretch; but, oh, the joy I've found in jumping on my own grave. I want you to know this joy, too.

Don't be afraid. Stand on your grave and jump for joy!

I affirm, brethren, by the boasting in you which
I have in Christ Jesus our Lord, I die daily.
1 Corinthians 15:31

Discover the immeasurable joy
of being taught by the Teacher.

TUESDAY

A Hungry Heart Is Intentional

I don't know about you, but I'm officially into birthday months. I decided long ago that a birth*day* was too short a celebration. I was already open to stretching it out for a week, but once I turned fifty I decided a full month was in order. It seems plumb crazy to think that I'm now more than a half century old, but you can't mess with math. (Which isn't exactly fair, because math is notorious for messing with me—but then I'm getting off topic earlier than usual.)

So, here's the deal. As I told my Twitter and Facebook friends, I've always heard that if you can make it to the age of fifty without growing up, you don't have to; and if that's the criteria, good Lord willing, I've got this, y'all! There's a great big world out there created by an even bigger and intensely personal God; and just like a little kid, I have questions, endless questions.

Here's the good part: God has all the answers. Jesus lived, suffered, died, and arose that we might call His Father ours, and I'm going to pursue everything I can know of Him and His ways until He takes me out of here. I've discovered the pure delight of asking a calculated "Why?" I'll read a verse of His good Word and say, "Why is that?" or "Why did that happen?" or "Why didn't that happen?" Why, why, why?

I know what you're wondering. Do I always get an answer? I absolutely do not. Father obviously has me on a need-to-know basis. But I'm addicted to the unequaled delight of having a thought settle in my heart that I can tie directly to another passage, and knowing deep down that I'm being taught by the Teacher who lives within me. There is no thrill like that thrill. If you don't know it, you need to—and I can give you a million reasons why.

If any of you lacks wisdom, you should ask God,
who gives generously to all without finding fault,
and it will be given to you.

JAMES 1:5 NIV

WEDNESDAY

A Hungry Heart Is Praying

Someone sent me a great video clip from *America's Funniest Videos*. I don't know if it won, but I would've given it first place. It stars an unhappy baby who is trying his best to have a fit but can't get any cooperation. As the clip opens, we see the baby throwing himself down on the floor and wailing. Only seconds later his audience, who is obviously the camera person, moves to another room. We can't see the baby now, but we can still hear him—until he stops crying. Slowly, however, he comes back into view, sniffling all the way. Once he relocates his audience, he falls out on the floor again, throwing a marvelous full-out hissy fit—at least until the camera leaves. Once again, this forces him to dry it up and go searching for his stage. The scene replays over and over again, and it gets funnier every time.

It also raises a very serious question. Tell me, what do you and I do with our sad times? It occurs to me that we big people sometimes look for audiences in the wrong places, too, or haven't you noticed? One of the most valuable lessons we can ever learn is to take our sad times to an audience of one, the One who sits on the throne. David, the shepherd boy who became a king, learned this lesson well. You can see it all through the Psalms.

David is the one who penned those famous words, "Weeping may endure for a night, but joy comes in the morning" (Psalm 30:5 NKJV). It's a familiar verse, but the key to it is found in the preceding verses, for while he was weeping, David was also crying out to the Lord. I believe the morning's joy was no automatic result, but a direct consequence of that decision.

It's vitally important that we seek the right audience and not let our weeping interfere with our sowing. We can have a pity party and refuse to sow our concerns in the right soil, but it's a poor choice indeed, for it will not only deny us of a harvest but leave us with only our misery for company. Let's not be like the poor little boy in the video. If we'll let go of our pain and bury it in prayer, we can bring forth sheaves of rejoicing.

Those who sow in tears shall reap in joy. He who continually goes forth weeping, bearing seed for sowing, shall doubtless come again with rejoicing, bringing his sheaves with him.
PSALM 126:5–6 NKJV

THURSDAY

A Hungry Heart Is Celebrating

I've discovered plenty of surprising things about aging that are less than pleasant. (I suppose I could use the word *maturing*, but I'm not sure it applies. So, there's that.) These findings of mine were not included in my southern mama's otherwise all-encompassing education, for reasons known only to she who is referred to in our family as the Queen of Us All, although I do have a theory. I mentioned it on my website if you're interested.

But back to my discoveries about aging. Some are probably universal, but I suspect that not all of them are, like my increasing tendency to let things slide in the housekeeping department. Due to that aforementioned education, I'm still fond of a neat house, and I continue to live by Mama's "pick it up and it won't pile up" rule, but the attention to detail around here is sorely lacking. Case in point: I recently used my sock foot to clean up a little slosh of coffee. I doubt the Queen has ever done such a thing. She may have a few years on me, but the Queen's house is usually cleaner than mine on my best day.

My point? I don't expect to win the Good Housekeeping Seal of Approval anytime soon. And you know what? I'm totally okay with that. I bear an infinitely better seal of approval, as does every other person who has been made new in Christ Jesus. All who have lost their lives to find them in Jesus have been sealed with the Holy Spirit of God.

One of the many varied blessings included in the promise of this heavenly seal is our acceptance at God's throne. You and I, believer, are as fully accepted and warmly welcomed before God's throne right now, today, whether new believer or seasoned saint, as we will be the day we stand before Him in heaven in our glorified bodies and sanctified souls. Grasping our favor with God through Christ is an immeasurably sweet truth that can yield great dividends in our faith. Savoring this access can lead us to deeper and closer communion with God than we would otherwise enjoy. And that is a discovery that is truly worthy of celebration!

> *Now He who establishes us with you in Christ*
> *and anointed us is God, who also sealed us and*
> *gave us the Spirit in our hearts as a pledge.*
> 2 CORINTHIANS 1:21–22

FRIDAY

A Hungry Heart Is Needy

I have a poor track record where taking medicine is concerned. It's a personal failing that should in no way be laid at the feet of the medical community. Many a good doctor has tried to reform me, bless their collective hearts, with little success. Before we go any further, I would like it noted that there have been at least two exceptions to this personal failing: their names are Jessica and Phillip. My medical misses did not apply to my offspring.

Back in the day, when it came time to administer meds to my kids, Mrs. Forgetful here turned into Doctor Do Right. I saw to it that the two of them got every dose, capsule, or vitamin they were ever prescribed. To be sure, the issue has always been one of me doctoring me. I know I should take the full round of prescribed antibiotics lest I invite a relapse, and I always mean to do just that, but once I start seeing improvements I'm prone to tapering off on the dosage.

Do you think my diligence in doling out my kids' prescriptions leaves me without excuse in my own hit-and-miss habit? I do, too, but I'm willing to bring it up anyway because I see a teachable moment for all of us who have a heart to follow Christ. As believers, we can fall victim to a similar erroneous mentality.

In the beginning, we'll run to Jesus like the sin-sick folks we are, filling our minds with His loving promises because they fall like balm on our aching souls. Only once we start "doing better" (for lack of a better description), we have the tendency to taper off in our dependence on Christ, unintentionally perhaps, unconsciously maybe, but the consequences are the same whether they are intentional or not. Slowly, our thoughts can turn less and less to Christ and more and more to the daily demands of what we call the real world. Can you say "relapse"?

Don't be lulled into the deception of self-sufficiency, dear Christian. Not only is Jesus the prescription for life, but we sorely need an ongoing IV of His sweet presence. Indeed, our greatest strength lies in knowing that we need Jesus today as much as we needed Him yesterday. We have no stores of grace in us. Our life is in Him. In Him alone are we whole.

The strongest believers become increasingly more dependent on Jesus, not less.

"I am the vine; you are the branches. If you
remain in me and I in you, you will bear
much fruit; apart from me you can do nothing."
JOHN 15:5 NIV

SATURDAY

A Hungry Heart Is Sharing

When the Thanksgiving and Christmas holidays begin to draw near, I begin setting my dining room table with my beautiful octagon-shaped Christmas china. It took me years to make this a practice!

For the longest time, I would marvel at the mint condition of my fine china's individual pieces on Christmas Day and make myself the same promise. *Next year I'm going to pull out the Christmas china earlier so we can enjoy its beauty longer.* I would tell myself that we should use the pretty gold-edged pieces from November through January. Myself would agree, too, but neither of us could remember our commitment by the time the next season rolled around. (I have found the voices in my head are good company, but they aren't always dependable in the help department.)

But back to the china. . . The very reason my holiday dishes are in such mint condition is because their days in the protected china cabinet far outweigh their days of service. They used to present a couple special holiday meals, along with a day or two of gumbo service for the bowls and sweets for the dessert plates, and that would be about it. Right back to the buffet they would go for storage. And that's why it is that, although my beautiful

Christmas china has been with the Tomlinson family for years, it doesn't have much to show for it.

On the other hand, the everyday stoneware in the kitchen has a story to tell with every chip and scratch. These pieces have been in the trenches, so to speak. It occurs to me that the trenches are where I want to be found, too. My goal is to live for Christ in the trenches of what we call this Christian walk. As believers, we're all called to be there.

I'm convinced that God isn't looking for fine china, all polished up, nick-free, and reserved with a prayer that He might use us for something big, something grand. Oh, that's not to say that He won't do something extraordinary with the yielded soul, but living our faith out loud in the ups and downs of our everyday lives is how we tell the redeeming story of His love.

Friends, let's determine to be highly useful everyday plates in the hands of our Father, all of our chips and scratches included. Fine china looks nice in the buffet, but everyday dishes, they tell the story!

We have this treasure in jars of clay to show that this
all-surpassing power is from God and not from us.
2 Corinthians 4:7 niv

MONDAY

A Hungry Heart Is Surrendered

The three of us had played school, read books, eaten snacks, and watched *Clifford the Big Red Dog*. This could only mean one thing. Church bells were ringing.

Playing church is high on my grandgirls' list when they come to Keggie's house, and that's fine by this belle. I'm all over it! Our services follow a predictable pattern, but they also have unique twists you won't necessarily find in your more traditional settings. We hold church in the piano room. I'm generally the pianist; Carlisle Mae leads the music; and her older sister, Emerson, brings the sermon. Emerson Ann is quite the fiery little preacher.

On the day I'm speaking of, then five-year-old Emerson was bringing one of her characteristically stirring messages, in which she likes to take a theme and hit it hard and often from all directions.

"We are God's sheep," she began. "And He is our Shepherd."

Emerson paused to stare at me. "Amen!" I said, belatedly. (In my defense, the song leader had just fallen and whacked her head on the piano bench. Someone had to give first aid.)

Pleased with my participation even if it was coerced, Emerson continued, reversing the order of her last point for emphasis. "He is our Shepherd," my granddaughter proclaimed. "And we are His sheep."

"Amen," I said, quickly this time. I said it several more times as she continued to hammer on her theme, until suddenly three-year-old Carlisle decided she'd recovered enough to preach. I brought this to the senior pastor's attention. For a minute I thought we might have a church split, but after a brief debate, Emerson begrudgingly introduced the visiting speaker.

Carlisle set her Bible at her feet and propped one foot on it (I can only surmise that she was standing on the promises). Then she pointed her finger at the congregation (me, Emerson, Froggy, and Bear) and announced, "We are His shepherd, and He is our sheep!"

I grinned when Carlisle Mae got it completely backward, but I couldn't help thinking that she totally nailed one of our biggest issues. I'm talking big believers now. We all are born with a desire to rule. If we can't rule the whole world, we at least want to rule our own domain. And yet the only way we will ever learn to reign in life is by kneeling. In the words of Senior Pastor Emerson Ann, "He is our Shepherd; we are His sheep."

Know that the LORD Himself is God;
It is He who has made us, and not we ourselves;
We are His people and the sheep of His pasture.
PSALM 100:3

TUESDAY

A Hungry Heart Is Intentional

One Christmas our number one son and his wife gave the beloved hubby and me a set of very nice and extremely sharp kitchen knives. The jokers around here entertained themselves discussing the wisdom of putting such knives in the hands of someone as easily distracted as yours truly. I couldn't help but laugh at their routine, even if it came at my own expense.

If we were a betting family, and we aren't, I have no doubt this group would also have laid down some friendly wagers as to how long it might be before I cut myself. And you know what bothers me the most about that, right? Some clown would've collected faster than quick.

I tried to be careful. I took my very healthy fear of those sharp new knives and I tried to avoid losing a finger. I made it about a week before the first accident. It wasn't bad, and I didn't sacrifice a digit, but blood was let and bandages were required.

Those supersharp knives have me thinking today of the sharp two-edged sword of God's Word. If we present ourselves before it, God will use His Word to cut away the hardened gray tissue of our hearts, revealing healthy pink flesh that beats for Him and pulses with the promise of eternal life. But it must be said: the same razor-sharp Word that brings healing to those who respect it and live by it will one day lay open every heart and bring judgment to those who have chosen not to heed it. Hear the sobering words of Revelation 19:15: "From His mouth comes a sharp sword, so that with it He may strike down the nations, and He will rule them with a rod of iron; and He treads the wine press of the fierce wrath of God, the Almighty."

Make no mistake, friend. There will be no safe way to handle that sword. Come, let's purpose to cultivate a healthy fear of the Word that we might discover the promises it holds for this life and escape the judgment it is sure to bring in the next.

For the word of God is living and active and sharper than any two-edged sword, and piercing as far as the division of soul and spirit, of both joints and marrow, and able to judge the thoughts and intentions of the heart.

HEBREWS 4:12

❧ WEDNESDAY ❧

A Hungry Heart Is Praying

I speak southern, heavy southern. For better or worse, this is the only voice I have. I couldn't get away from it if I tried. My voice comes with me, and by all accounts it seems to linger when I'm gone. I've had people tell me they hear my voice when they're reading my columns or my books. Poor things. That makes me want to apologize for being in their personal space.

People tend to recognize me by my voice quicker than they do by my appearance, too. It's not unusual to meet someone around these parts and have them say something like, "Hey! You're Everything Southern!" or "I know you. You're the All Southern Girl." But nine times out of ten this happens after we have exchanged greetings, and not before. I see no need to correct 'em on the actual title. If they're anywhere close to All Things Southern, I consider it a win.

Of course it's worth noting that I've been on the radio for more than a decade now, at least in northeast Louisiana. My point? The people recognizing my voice are those who've been exposed to it on a regular basis. My voice is identifiable to them only to the extent that it has become familiar to them. There's an eternal truth here for all who will hear it, and thankfully it has nothing to do with this southern twang of mine.

We all long to hear from God. (Don't even try to be the odd man out and tell me that you wouldn't stop on a dime if you heard the God of the universe speak to you; because frankly, I won't believe you.) So why is it that so many people live their lives without hearing and recognizing His voice? I'd like to humbly suggest that it's because we often fail to listen for Him. God speaks. He speaks through nature, He speaks through His Word, and He speaks to our spirits. Recognizing His voice is about setting our hearts on His channel and choosing His instruction as our go-to Source, listening for Him today and tomorrow and the day after that until we come to know the voice that calms the waters and soothes our souls.

> *"Call to me and I will answer you, and will tell you*
> *great and hidden things that you have not known."*
> JEREMIAH 33:3 ESV

When we turn to Christ,
He forgets our past and
renames us for our future.

THURSDAY

A Hungry Heart Is Celebrating

My old schoolmates and I paid our last respects to one of our own, hugged her grieving family again, and sloshed through the muddy graveyard. We felt much older, and yes, a little bit wiser than we were at our last class reunion. It was the second time we'd stood by the grave of a high school buddy, and we knew it wouldn't be the last. As the rest of the funeral-goers began to make their way out of the cemetery, our small group began to converge into a tight circle near our vehicles. Ever so slowly we began to relive the past, all of us reaching for something solid and familiar, the way people do when they need to steady themselves.

The guys joked about their thinning hair and bulging middles and commented on how much kinder time had been to the girls. We women grinned and sang the praises of the cosmetic industry and the wonder of our morning makeovers.

It's funny, regardless of who we become after high school, those years seem to mark us forever in one another's eyes. Some people will always remember you as the one who toilet-papered the teachers' houses and left spoiled eggs on their doorsteps. Not that I know anyone who did that! Right. If your past contains things you'd rather forget, I have some great news from the Good Book that you're sure to enjoy as much as I have.

Upon being introduced to Andrew's brother, Jesus looked at the man who would one day be known the world over for his infamous betrayal and said, "'You are Simon the son of Jonah. You shall be called Cephas' (which is translated, A Stone)" (John 1:42 NKJV).

Did you see that? Jesus saw who Peter was and who Peter would be. That's good, but it gets better! Peter's actions may have forever colored his reputation in our eyes, but not in the eyes of his Master. Please note that Jesus didn't name Peter by his betrayal. He named Peter by his belief: "'You shall be called Cephas' (which is translated, A Stone)."

If we've been born again, we have new names, too. It's not what others call us; and our new name doesn't allude to mistakes some might not let us forget. Crank up a praise song, and let's celebrate!

See what great love the Father has lavished
on us, that we should be called children
of God! And that is what we are!
1 JOHN 3:1 NIV

A Hungry Heart Is Needy

When we were growing up on the end of Bull Run Road, my sisters and I spent many a Saturday accompanying Mama to Tallulah, Louisiana, mostly against our will, to buy groceries and supplies for the coming week. We would've preferred running hog wild in the fields that surrounded our house or playing Chase Don't Touch the Ground on the farm equipment under Papa's shed. We considered splitting precious daylight hours between the A&P and TG&Y and then traveling home again to unload and put away the supplies to be a form of torture.

Our lack of enthusiasm probably contributed to Mama's habit of making sure we didn't leave home without hearing her favorite warning: "I expect you girls to behave today."

In retrospect, I suppose it was a reasonable expectation, given the continuing education course Mama was always putting us through on the many things little ladies did and did not do. We girls understood full well that we should behave, and we knew what it meant to behave, but it wasn't unusual for us to run out of resolve way before Mama ran out of errands.

That childhood memory makes me smile, but it also gives me cause to celebrate Father God's marvelous provision for you and me in Christ Jesus. Color me exceedingly grateful that God doesn't begin His work in us as believers by telling us to behave. The law did a stellar good job of proving that we don't know how, which came as no surprise to God. In fact, according to the apostle Paul, the law came for that very reason—to teach us how desperately needy we are and to prepare us for the saving work of Christ.

On this side of the cross, God asks us to believe and trust in Jesus so we can behave—through the power of His Holy Spirit, the hope of glory, living through us. And then He asks us to keep our eyes on Jesus and keep believing so that we can keep on behaving.

Our blessed takeaway? Through His amazing grace, Father God has made it so that He can say, "I expect you to behave today," and you and I are equipped to comply. Somebody needs to say, "Hallelujah!"

For sin shall not be master over you,
for you are not under law but under grace.

ROMANS 6:14

A Hungry Heart Is Sharing

Do you remember grade school romance and trusted friends bearing sweaty notes from secret admirers with little boxes drawn with a number two pencil? "Do you like me? Check yes or no." Those days are sitting fresh in my memory due to a certain itty-bitty who recently laid her vulnerable heart open and told me about the man of her dreams, who I'm sure is all of seven. My heart swelled with hers. It was a tender conversation that left me thinking about another love note, a divine one. Go with me, if you will, to the wilderness of Sinai. The Israelites have set up camp at the base of Mount Horeb, even as their ever-faithful, ever-attentive God settled in at its peak and promptly invited Moses up to His place for a get-together.

There God instructs Moses to remind the people of how He brought them out of Egypt unto Himself. And then He promises that if they will obey Him and keep His covenant, they will be His chosen possession. We can find a word-for-word account in Exodus 19, but if you'll allow me some freedom, God's incredible invitation could be loosely translated, "If you'll be mine, I'll be yours."

Message in hand, Moses brought God's words to the people.

Scripture tells us they listened as God's ambassador read His letter, and then they pledged to be faithful to His commandments. Only they didn't. They couldn't. Nor can we. Not under the strength of our own good intentions, we can't.

Enter sweet Jesus.

Moses, you see, was a type of Christ. He was a picture of the Friend who sticks closer than a brother—only Jesus was sent to earth on a heavenly mission bearing a better love note. Through Jesus, an invitation to be God's own people was renewed. Only this time, Jesus Himself pledged to fulfill our end of the deal if we would put our faith and trust in Him. Now that's a story that doesn't get old, and one we should never tire of telling. See Jesus now, taking our hands and putting them back into His Father's. Let's share the greatest story ever told so others can say yes to Him, and we can all shout, "Amen!"

God was in Christ reconciling the world to Himself,
not counting their trespasses against them.
2 CORINTHIANS 5:19

A Hungry Heart Is Surrendered

I'm sitting on pins and needles waiting for the phone to ring. I'm expecting a conference call, a fairly important one, any minute now. Three of us will be on the line with one subject on our minds. We'll all be testing the waters in our own ways and trying to determine if a partnership between us would be a good fit. Should we or should we not work together on that looming project?

Forgive me if I sound vague. This is one of those things a belle needs to keep close to her chest until the deal is done or not done. The phone call I'm so excited about could lead to some very good news, or the trial balloon could pop just as quickly as it was inflated and disappear into thin air. Only time will tell. Well, that's not entirely true. I'll tell, too, sooner or later. It's a given.

I've had this type of phone conversation/interview before, so I pretty much know what to expect. Past experience leads me to believe everyone will be very polite but no one will actually commit to anything and no one will show their full hand. It's the way business relationships work, and I don't suppose there's anything wrong with that. On the other hand, there's one place where such a hedge-your-bet type of attitude absolutely will not work for you. This would be experience talking, too.

No one discovers an intimate, life-transforming relationship with God by testing the notion of following Him without ever fully committing. You can bank on it. We'll never know the fullness of a life lived in Christ unless we are all in. Meeting Him isn't a blind date type of get-together with each party checking the other one out. The business world and the dating world may teach us not to burn our bridges, but I've found that when answering God's holy call, blowing up the bridge behind my commitments is the only way to roll. (Ladies, think of it as throwing away your fat pants!)

I heartily suggest going all in! You'll never regret it. I have more to say about burning bridges, but we'll have to save it. I think I hear the phone!

Our God is a consuming fire.
Hebrews 12:29

A Hungry Heart Is Intentional

Experience had taught me that I was on shaky ground, so I proceeded cautiously. "You let Cyndie go when she was my age," I said, as respectfully as possible. Those teenage years are long gone, but how well I remember lobbying Mama for special requests. It was a delicate science at best, and I was playing my whole hand by trying to establish the big-sister precedent. There was always the chance that Mama might come back with a ruling in my favor. However, if she already regretted letting her oldest child do whatever it was I wanted to do, the only thing I was likely to get would be an icy-cold stare and a "Is your name Cyndie?" type of question. Game over.

Years later my own kids played the precedent card, too. They were prone to lock onto whatever I granted once as a verifiable new pattern, set in stone. Isn't it interesting that even little kids have a built-in understanding of precedents? Oh, the word may be foreign and the chances of their being able to define it slim to none, but our tots master this game early on and without any explanation or assistance. You can see it in a variety of ways. For instance, I've noticed my girls being very careful about my grandbabies' naptimes and schedules. They're trying to avoid starting anything they don't want to continue, like, say, rocking a baby for an hour and a half to try to get the wee one to nap instead of letting the infants learn to put themselves to sleep. (I bet you can figure out which method I used!)

When I see things that are so deeply ingrained in our common human DNA, like our affinity for precedents, my brain immediately goes to the One who programmed us. If we're so obviously wired to be precedent-setting people, that characteristic must have a purpose. I wonder what it could be.

This is hardly a definitive theory, but here's what I'm thinking. God revealed Himself through Jesus Christ. The life of Christ is full of precedents that tell us who God is and how He will act in the present and future based on what He did or said in the past. Earthly parents may live to regret a precedent because they have second-guessed an earlier decision, but our God never makes mistakes in judgment that He would like to forget. Maybe that's why He wired us to look for His precedents. Of course, you can't stand on these precedents unless you know them, and you can't know them unless you read the Book!

Jesus Christ is the same yesterday and today and forever.
HEBREWS 13:8

A Hungry Heart Is Praying

My best friend and I recently discovered Dubsmash, and we've been creating tons of fun little video clips and texting them back and forth in the name of entertainment. Granted, we're way behind the rest of the world with our discovery of this cool little app that lets you lip sync snatches of songs and other silly lines, but we don't care. When we find something that makes us laugh, we wear it out.

I particularly love Dubsmash, because people like me who can't carry a tune in a bucket with two hands can lip sync our way to superstardom, at least in our own minds. All you have to do is choose a lyric, hit RECORD, and you're ready to send your masterpiece. That's the goal, anyway. Did I mention Dubsmash is an addictive time drainer? Yes. When I first discovered Dubsmash, I'd set out to tape one funny little clip for Red and I'd get sucked in, taping and retaping, all to better sync my lips to the tape. But practice makes perfect. These days I can mimic someone else's words without much effort at all. Which is fine, I suppose, as long as we're talking Dubsmash.

It occurs to me that sometimes we believers have a similar tendency to use someone else's words when we approach God in prayer, and that's not good at all. Lines and phrases we've heard all our lives can work their way into our prayers. Some of us who have been churched and rechurched can offer an entire prayer of someone else's familiar words without once involving our own hearts.

Jesus had a lot to say about such prayers. If you'll allow me to summarize, beware the prayers of repetition that don't involve the heart. It's false repentance. Let's be raw, be real, and be heard.

> *"When you are praying, don't say meaningless things like the unbelievers do, because they think they will be heard by being so wordy."*
>
> MATTHEW 6:7 ISV

THURSDAY

A Hungry Heart Is Celebrating

Did you ever see that commercial about the monk trying his best to be in perfect harmony with nature? It's an oldie that makes me smile in a "I remember doing that" sort of way. Oh, not the part where he turns over that sweet turtle that's trapped on its back, although I would definitely do that! And not the part where he scoops up a spider indoors and releases it safely outdoors. (I would never do that!) No, the part that I identify with is when the poor monk reaches for a tissue and blows his nose, only to shrink back in horror as he reads the words printed on the box. There, in bold print, is the proud announcement that Kleenex Anti-Viral Tissue traps and kills 99.9 percent of cold and flu viruses. Kills them. As the commercial trails off, the monk looks heavenward as an unseen voice says, "Thank goodness for forgiveness. Thank goodness for Kleenex tissue."

There was a time when my twisted thinking had me living much like that monk. I was trapped in my own careful efforts to avoid sin as a way to please God. I had long since given my life to God, but I continued to battle endlessly to live out my faith and walk daily with my Savior. However big or small the failure, there was always something I had or had not done that was waiting there to trip me up, to make me feel distanced from my Father. And of course, that mind-set supplied my enemy with yet another opportunity to holler, "Gotcha!"

These days you'll find me spending almost an equal amount of time thanking the Father for teaching me how to enjoy this precious faith as I do thanking Him for my salvation. I now live in the assurance of 1 John 1:7, that Jesus keeps me and cleanses me when I'm following hard after Him: "If we walk in the light as He is in the light, we have fellowship with one another, and the blood of Jesus Christ His Son cleanses us from all sin" (NKJV).

Is such thinking a license to do whatever I will? Hardly. On the contrary, knowing we're eternally welcome at the throne through Jesus is an open invitation to come and dine with the Master. It's an assurance that beckons us closer, 24-7. Pass the tissues, friend. These are tears of joy!

For you were formerly darkness, but now you are
Light in the Lord; walk as children of Light.

EPHESIANS 5:8

A Hungry Heart Is Needy

I was just a child the first time I heard it said that a good woman could throw more out the back door than a good man could bring in through the front. For the life of me, I couldn't imagine why the man's wife wanted to throw all of their stuff in the backyard. Years later I realized that the front door–back door visual was a way of saying that the woman was being wasteful. I got that.

I was raised by people who believed in being good stewards of God's great blessings, and I agreed with the theory even if I didn't always appreciate the practices they employed. Conservation isn't so attractive when you're the youngest of three little tomboys and your mother is always reminding your sisters to "save the bathwater!" I envied Cyndie getting to take that first sparkling-clean dip.

I would imagine you have similar stories. We've all been told to "waste not, want not," and we've been cautioned that "a penny saved is a penny earned." This from well-meaning people hoping to teach us that we could get ahead instead of scraping by if only we'd be careful to save what we had in hand. Scrimping and saving is great economic advice, my friends, but it is poor practice in our spiritual lives. We need to reprogram our thinking where it concerns our walk with Christ. I'll explain.

All the wonderful graces of our sweet Jesus have been given to us. We can take all we want, but we must be willing to come back to Him over and over to receive. Come and receive, come and receive, it's the only way we can experience the abundant life that is Christ in us, living through us.

We waste-not, want-not people must learn that it's impossible to use the graces of Christ economically and make them last. We can't stockpile who He is and parse Him out to those around us. If we try to find the goodness, mercy, grace, patience, forgiveness, faithfulness, and kindness of Christ in our own dispositions, we'll be sorely disappointed every time. There is nothing good in us apart from Christ, but we're welcome to draw on the bank of heaven with every breath we take. He is an inexhaustible well, willing to fill our leaking cisterns today and tomorrow.

If this were a group session, I might say it this way: "Hello, my name is Shellie. I'm a spiritual pauper living hand to mouth on the words of God."

"Ho! Every one who thirsts, come to the waters;
and you who have no money come, buy and eat. Come,
buy wine and milk without money and without cost."

Isaiah 55:1

Let's put people on our bucket
list in this world and live
to see them in the next.

SATURDAY

A Hungry Heart Is Sharing

I have a theory and a disclaimer. The disclaimer first: my theory isn't doctrinal, and you won't find it anywhere in scripture, so don't go looking. Actually, it's not even a theory. That sounds like something I'd need to prove. This is more of a notion, but I'm fond of it, and quite naturally that makes me want to share it with y'all.

I think the time is coming when I will get to lay my eyes on every wonder of creation in this whole wide world. From Kilimanjaro in Tanzania to the Great Barrier Reef in Australia, from the Angel Falls of Venezuela to the Dead Sea of the Jordan, from the Amazon in South America to the Underground River of the Philippines, I'm thinking I'll get to see them all in a land called eternity. Oh, yes, I knew you'd need a bit more explanation, and I'm happy to oblige.

As I study God's Word, I find myself struck more and more by His tendency to speak in types and shadows. The Bible is full of references to things on earth that mimic things in heaven. So consider this: What if everything we see is only an imitation of a heavenly model we will one day behold? What if, right? The thought will take your breath away if you let it.

Again, I'm not teaching a new doctrine, folks, just giving you a peek into my recent thinking. I wanted to mention it because of what the theory has done for me. In short, it's encouraged me to swap the idea of a bucket list, an itemized dream of what I'd like to do before I leave this world, for a record of who I'd like to take with me into the next. My new bucket list now reads with line items like, "Let the love of Jesus be so fully expressed through my life that others are drawn to Him like moths to a flame!" How about that? Let's all put people on our bucket list. It could be that we'll get to see those Angel Falls together!

"Let your light shine before men in such
a way that they may see your good works,
and glorify your Father who is in heaven."

MATTHEW 5:16

While the good woman boasts
and the failed woman hides,
the surrendered woman finds hope.

MONDAY

A Hungry Heart Is Surrendered

I have a reputation in my immediate circle that's well earned. I'm forgetful in a uniquely selective way. I can't remember to buy milk at the grocery store, but I can access childhood memories, random song lyrics, and an untold number of stories in my head at will. My man has always said that my brain needs to be devoted to science when I check out of here. I'm okay with that as long as y'all make sure that I'm completely through using it.

By the way, before you waste your valuable time sending me tips and links on how to improve my memory, I should tell you that I've read all the articles and I've used all the prompts. I already take notes in my smartphone. And then I forget my smartphone. I already know to make lists. I've even made lists of my lists, but that doesn't keep them on my brain's cluttered little desktop. Clearly, I have a limited amount of space up there, and my system has its own priorities on what should be stored and what needs to be deleted.

My point: I don't intentionally have to practice that type of forgetfulness. I'm something of a natural expert. On the other hand, there's a completely different sort of forgetfulness that I regularly have to remind myself to practice. What's more, I've found this type of forgetfulness to be of extreme importance in my pursuit of Christ.

I'm talking about self-forgetfulness, or what I like to think of as refusing to get stuck in the muck of me. See, it's as foolish to feel that I can approach God because of what I've done right as it is to feel like God is unapproachable because of what I've done wrong.

I must forget me entirely. To walk with Christ, you must do the same. The only way any of us can approach this holy God is through the door that is Jesus, our mediator.

Self-forgetfulness before God comes with great rewards! I never experience His healing presence when I come to Him feeling like a good woman nor when I hide from Him because I feel like a failed woman. I find healing, forgiveness, and restoration when I come to Jesus as a desperate, fully surrendered woman who knows Christ Jesus is my only hope.

My soul, wait in silence for God only,
for my hope is from Him.
PSALM 62:5

TUESDAY

A Hungry Heart Is Intentional

Oh, how well I remember the cool autumn afternoons of my youth. My sisters and I couldn't get our school clothes changed into our play clothes and get outside fast enough to suit us. Sometimes we got to go to the fields to stomp cotton for Papa. Other times there'd be a trailer of cotton calling to us from under Papa's equipment shed. Now, that was fun! In the field, playing was mixed with working as we had to make sure the cotton was stomped good before Papa came back by with another load. A trailer of cotton under the shed, however, was wide open for hours of unstructured imaginative play. We'd jump, dive, and dig in that cotton until our stomachs worked up a healthy appetite and started growling, signaling suppertime and more of Mama's good country cooking.

The only problem was mealtime didn't run on our schedule. It ran on Mama's, regardless of how many times we went to the kitchen door to ask that age-old question, "When will dinner be ready?" My belly is aching just thinking about it. It didn't matter how hungry we were; we weren't eating until Mama put the food on the table and called us in. I don't remember the specific day I realized that I was old enough to decide it was lunchtime whenever I wanted it to be lunchtime, but I can tell you that I like it, and I imagine you do, too. Growing up sure has its advantages!

So, tell me. Have you grown up spiritually since you first believed in Jesus, or are you still waiting for others to feed you out of God's Word? The glory of Immanuel, God with us, is that we don't have to be dependent on others for a word that will feed us—that will lift our spirits and bring comfort during stressful circumstances. The Bread of Life has been prepared for all eternity. Come on, folks. Let's open our Bibles, grow up, and feed ourselves.

I gave you milk to drink, not solid food;
for you were not yet able to receive it.
Indeed, even now you are not yet able.

1 Corinthians 3:2

A Hungry Heart Is Praying

My readers and radio listeners probably feel like they know me pretty well—and they may be right. I'm kind of an open book. For instance, if you're a regular reader, you know I like toe popping (there's a story there), fried catfish, and chocolate Labs. You've heard me talk about my three big passions: faith, friends, and family. You've heard me invite you to my cyber porch time and again to swap stories. I appreciate those of you who have taken me up on it (and I'm still wondering where the rest of you are!). And yet as hard as it might be to believe, I don't tell you everything. Sorry. It's not that I don't care about y'all. I do. It's just that you and I are never really alone.

We may e-mail back and forth; we may visit via my column in the Saturday paper; we may chat on the radio, in the pages of a local magazine, or on one of the hot social networking sites. If so, I truly appreciate you, but the bottom line is, we're always in a crowd, the two of us, and a crowd has built-in intimacy issues.

Granted, it's not all that unusual for us not to bare our souls to each other. Most normal people (and by "normal" I mean those who aren't desperate for their fifteen minutes of fame) draw lines between those things they're willing to discuss in public and those subjects they reserve for private talks. Intimate discussions are an authentic mark of all close relationships.

Think about it. Who among us hasn't caught the eye of a close friend and exchanged the look that means, "We'll talk about this again when we're alone." That's what I thought. Now that we're on the same page, let me tell you about the scripture passage that has me thinking along these lines. In these verses, Jesus and His closest friends are retiring from a crowded place. The part that has my attention today is that found in Mark 4:34: "When they were alone, He explained all things to His disciples" (NKJV).

Jesus has a lot of things to say to the casual crowd, but he has so much more for the sincere follower. Man says, "Reveal yourself to me, and I will seek you." God says, *"Seek Me, and I will reveal Myself to you."* We can find Him in the crowd; but to know Him, to enjoy His sweet fellowship, we're going to need to draw aside.

> *"Ask, and it will be given to you; seek, and you*
> *will find; knock, and it will be opened to you."*
> MATTHEW 7:7

THURSDAY

A Hungry Heart Is Celebrating

The young man who stopped by our table could not have been smiling any broader. Having heard that he was recently engaged, and having noted that he was with an attractive young lady we hadn't had the pleasure of meeting, my husband and I were fairly certain we knew who was responsible for his big, cheesy grin.

Phil and I exchanged greetings with the couple, and we all began to make small talk. During our conversation, our young friend continued to smile broadly as he looked at his date, back at us, and back at her again. We could tell he was very eager to share his good news with us, if only he could figure out how. I was trying to decide if I should help him out by bringing up the subject myself when his sweetheart nodded good-bye and turned as if to join their friends waiting at the checkout counter. Something about her move jolted her intended into action, and out came one of the sweetest, most gleeful wedding announcements I've heard in a long time.

"I'm going to marry her!" he proclaimed proudly. His joyful news was clear, concise, and charming to the max.

It was also endearing to my man and me, as it brought back sweet memories of when we were young and enjoying the early days of our own courtship. Several days later I was running some scripture references when I thought yet again about the young man's obvious enthusiasm.

Isaiah 62:5 reads, "As a bridegroom rejoices over his bride, so will your God rejoice over you" (NIV). The New Testament book of John identifies Jesus as that happy bridegroom, while Revelation describes the marriage supper of the Lamb that He is joyfully anticipating. It's all part of a heavenly wedding that will eclipse any ceremony this earth has ever seen. It may be hard for you and me to grasp, but according to God's Word, the very thought delights the heart of God. It's as if a most joyful announcement has gone forth in glory: "He's going to marry us!"

What's more, while the groom-to-be in my story may have been somewhat at a loss for words, Jesus never is. Let's revel in the tailor-made proposal He continues to spread far and wide. It's clear, concise, and charming to the max.

And the very best part? It goes out to "whoever desires."

And the Spirit and the bride say, "Come!" And let him
who hears say, "Come!" And let him who thirsts come.
Whoever desires, let him take the water of life freely.
REVELATION 22:17 NKJV

A Hungry Heart Is Needy

The grandgirls and I were on our way to their swimming lessons. Five-year-old Emerson was excited. Three-year-old Carlisle, not so much. Her mommy had told me about the previous day's lesson so that I would be prepared, but Carlisle gave me her own version of a heads-up as we were pulling in the drive.

"Keggie," she said, "I'm going to cry some, and then I'm going to calm down."

Bless it. Carlisle was thinking ahead. Yesterday's experience was fresh on her little heart. She fully expected to get scared, which is why she was anticipating a meltdown, but she was also determining how to deal with it. I love that. I think we can learn from it.

Regardless of what stage of life we're in, the future can be intimidating. We can fear for our health, and we can worry about our job security. We can fear growing older, and we can be fearful about our children growing older and facing who-knows-what-kind of world. What we need not do is let our fears morph into oversized monsters that paralyze us in the present. Carlisle knew the swimming instructor would be right there with her, and we know that Jesus has promised never to leave us nor forsake us.

What's more, instead of letting the "what-ifs" of the looming lesson terrorize her, Carlisle was making a plan for getting to the other side of the trauma. What if we were that brave? Secret fears lose their power when they're exposed to the light. What if we took a page from Carlisle's book? What if we could learn to say, "If the Lord doesn't answer my prayer the way I want Him to, if the thing I don't want to happen happens, I'm going to cry my ever-loving eyes out. Then I'm going to calm down and rest my needy heart in the arms of my God, for He is faithful."

I think it would be the difference between really living and balancing on one foot, waiting for the other to fall. Put that way, it doesn't sound like a choice at all.

> *But as for me, I trust in You,*
> *O LORD, I say, "You are my God."*
> PSALM 31:14

A Hungry Heart Is Sharing

I was eight, I think. I was scared—this I know for a fact. The well-dressed woman in front of me appeared nice enough, but she was a complete stranger, and our one-on-one meeting had all the cozy feel of the principal's office. My sisters and I were being formally adopted so that we could bear the name of the only man whom I had ever considered my dad, the one who had long ago stepped in and chosen the role.

After explaining what I already knew, that she needed to ask me some questions before the judge could make a ruling, the stranger leaned in like the two of us were best friends having a conspiratorial conversation and quietly asked, "So, Shellie, do you want Ed Rushing to be your daddy?" This was some question to ask an eight-year-old, but at least I had been prepared for it by my sisters. Their turns had come first. "Yes'm," I said, eager to wrap up our little get-together. Case closed, right? Wrong.

My one-word answer didn't seem to satisfy my interviewer. She pushed on. "But why? Why do you want him to be your daddy?" Was she joking? Did she really expect an answer? I wanted to tell her that it was a stupid question as he already was my daddy, but I didn't dare. We girls weren't allowed to use the *s* word, much less address it toward an adult. I stopped short and thought hard. "Because I like him," I said. Only my matter-of-fact pronouncement came out "yike him" due to my ever-present childhood speech impediment. Later, Miss Voice of the State shared my answer with my parents, who found it endearing. My older sisters, of course, found it perfect fodder for teasing me unmercifully. "Because I yike him" would henceforth and forever be a part of our family lore.

Friends, "I yike him" served its purpose when I was eight, but as a disciple of Jesus Christ, I'm expected to have a better answer prepared for those who ask why I believe as I do. I've accepted that challenge. Will you?

Always be prepared to give an answer to everyone who asks you to give the reason for the hope that you have.
1 PETER 3:15 NIV

A Hungry Heart Is Surrendered

Someone sent me a video clip of the sweetest marriage proposal. It opens with a young man singing a love song to his sweetie. Suddenly another fellow appears. This one dances into view while lip-syncing joyfully to the tune. Then another dancer arrives, and another, as a theme begins to emerge. The intimate moment turns into a full-out celebration. As the boy guides his sweetheart along a marked path, their loved ones appear from all directions performing solos, duets, and quartets. The girlfriend has clearly figured out what the budding musical is about and who is behind it, but she is still reeling by the size of the cast, which includes many friends and both sets of parents. The growing parade ends on the beach with her beau on his knee. Of course I cried.

Afterward I scanned the comments below the video. The women were swooning. The men were protesting good-naturedly that the young man had set the bar way too high! Then I saw it, the comment that has stayed with me. One woman typed, "It was nice, but the music was too high." Really? That was her takeaway? All of that love and friendship on display, and she chose to complain about the volume? It reminded me of what Jesus once said to the religious people who were hammering John for being a wild man who refused to eat and drink while they criticized Jesus for dining with publicans and sinners. Jesus said, "To what shall I compare this generation? It is like children sitting in the market places, who call out to the other *children*, and say, 'We played the flute for you, and you did not dance; we sang a dirge, and you did not mourn'" (Matthew 11:16–17).

Jesus depicted these petulant, childish people who refused to accept the Gospel, regardless of its presentation, as sitting in the marketplace. Interesting. A fickle culture craving endless entertainment—now, where have we seen that before? Oh, right! How vain it is to try and please this world. Whatever we do, someone won't like it, someone else will demand that we top it, and the bar will be raised another notch. May I recommend instead a life given over to Christ? It means full acceptance with God, and it is based on Jesus' merits and not our next great performance. Someone needs to say amen!

To the praise of the glory of his grace,
wherein he hath made us accepted in the beloved.
EPHESIANS 1:6 KJV

A Hungry Heart Is Intentional

The picture got my attention first. I was scrolling through a feed on a news website when I saw it, a bronze statue of a lady sitting on the front row of a beautiful church with what appeared to be an open Bible on her lap. Beside her sat a flesh-and-blood woman with a smile on her face and an arm around the frozen one's shoulders. Now that was interesting, but the accompanying article was unbelievable. In it, the statue was described as the embalmed and bronzed image of a longtime churchgoer who was so devoted to her spot in the pew that her family received special permission to bronze her body and affix it permanently to her special aisle seat where she had sat for the previous forty years.

Talk about being stuck in the pew! I was knee deep googling all the related articles and getting quite a picture of the divide it was causing in the church between those members who thought it was sweet and those who found it unsettling, when I realized I'd been had. Yes, it was a gag, and I had fallen for it along with several million other people. Have mercy!

And yet here's the hard truth. It happens all the time. Oh, not the bronzed version of a die-hard church member, but something similar. It's all too easy for any of us to get stuck in our comfy spot. It happens when we swallow the ridiculous deception that having been born again, we know enough about this mysterious all-powerful amazing God and the only thing that remains for us is "to do church" till we die. Can I be honest? That's seriously off-putting to me. It also nails me, because I once lived that way and I was well on my way to atrophying in my pew.

I've come to understand that a choice always lies before us. We can sit fixed and immovable year in and year out with hearts as hard as a bronze statue, or we can regularly and deliberately lay our hearts bare and ask this God-man, this Savior, this Messiah to make them burn again. If you choose the latter, get ready. He is a consuming fire.

> *Therefore, since we are receiving a kingdom that cannot*
> *be shaken, let us be thankful, and so worship God acceptably*
> *with reverence and awe, for our "God is a consuming fire."*
> HEBREWS 12:28–29 NIV

When we lose our fake church
language, we find the listening
ear of a very real God.

A Hungry Heart Is Praying

I was teaching from the book of Hosea when I made a personal confession to the girls in my Sunday school class and illustrated it with an example from my own prayer life. I share it because you may get a chuckle out of it like they did, and I like to say that life is better when you're laughing. Besides, it comes with a great lesson.

Sometimes I find myself praying without saying anything. Indeed, I can take words and phrases I've heard from other folks' prayers and string them together in a nice-sounding prayer while being totally unengaged in the result. Worse still, sometimes I catch myself saying ridiculous things while I'm praying that suggests my mouth may still be in DRIVE but my brain has gone into PARK or wandered onto a side road.

Just last week I was enjoying a truly delightful prayer time when my brain went AWOL and I heard myself say, "Oh, Lord God, I am Your refuge."

Really, Shellie? Do you suppose the Lord laughed out loud with that great cloud of witnesses in heaven? Perhaps Gabriel turned to Him and said, "And what do you need to hide from, exactly?"

My brain cramp was embarrassing, but at least I've learned

not to accept the enemy's condemnation about such things anymore. I don't give up these days. I just steer myself back on the road. That's progress right there.

While you're getting a laugh at my expense, I'll move on to the lesson I mentioned. In Hosea 14:2 we hear God tell His people to "Take words with you and return to the LORD." In the original Hebrew language, that verse can be read, "Take realities with you and return to the LORD."

Now isn't that interesting? A reality is defined as "something that is rather than something as you want it to be or imagine it to be." Sounds like God wants us to lose our church language and woolgathering and get real with Him. As I look around at the state of our world, I make a fresh commitment to do just that, and I hope you'll join me. If not now, when?

Take words with you and return to the LORD.
Say to Him, "Take away all iniquity and receive us
graciously, that we may present the fruit of our lips."
HOSEA 14:2

THURSDAY

A Hungry Heart Is Celebrating

My heart went out to the adorable little girl in the tiny swimsuit. She was all of three years old, and she was not happy, not one bit. It appeared she had no plans to get happy either—at least not during swimming lessons. She was crying when she arrived with her grandmother, and she refused all consolation during the lesson.

But here's the curious part. When it came time for her to get off the steps at the shallow end and take a turn with the teacher, the little swimmer stopped crying. She also took a breath, put her face in the water, and used her arms and legs exactly like she was instructed with nary a tear or sniffle! Considering her despair about the whole thing, I was surprised to see that she was quite capable. I was even more surprised at what happened next. I had assumed the tears were over. No, ma'am. That sweet child repeated that sequence throughout the thirty-minute class. She would cry mournfully on the sideline, compose herself in the water, and resume crying as soon as she was returned to the steps.

As I watched the other swimmers around her giggling and splashing water, I thought about the striking lesson before me. Life is full of days we want no part of and circumstances we flat-out dread. Sometimes, like our little swimmer, we can decide if we're unhappy, overworked, or mistreated and refuse to budge from that position. We can complain about what we've been through and dread what's coming next so much that we fail to enjoy our lives in and around the challenges. That's a sad state of affairs for those living in rebellion against God; for believers to carry on so when Jesus has promised to be with us now and forever is beyond tragic. Oh, that we would celebrate God's past provision and protection and allow such memories of His faithfulness to fortify us against tomorrow's tasks. Life is happening *now*. Let's enjoy it.

> *This is the day that the LORD has made;*
> *let us rejoice and be glad in it.*
> PSALM 118:24 ESV

FRIDAY

A Hungry Heart Is Needy

The young woman standing in front of me was going to be boarding the same plane on which I was about to travel while her sweetie was flying out of a different gate, to another destination. The two of them were trying to part ways, but the impending separation was proving to be too difficult for them. Standing toe to toe and holding hands, they'd give each other a quick peck on the lips, and then he would try and walk off, only he couldn't get two feet away before he turned around on his own accord or she called him back. Either way, the scene would begin again with them staring deep into each other's eyes.

As the scene played out, I could tell some of the folks around us were growing uncomfortable. I wasn't. Their passion wasn't bothering me at all. Oh, sure, the lovebirds' affection was on public display, but I didn't feel like they were crossing the line. I found them totally charming. If anything, they made my own heart grow tender thinking about getting home to my hardworking farmer.

As I watched the love-struck couple, I wondered about the thoughts of those around me. It occurred to me that there was probably someone or a couple of someones in the couple's unintended audience who were watching the couple for completely different reasons. Perhaps there was someone watching who had never known a love like the one on display, someone who before that day was skeptical that such a love even existed. If so, I promise you this, the lovebirds would have shaken that person's conviction to its core.

I can divide my life into the dispassionate years I spent knowing of Jesus but not loving Jesus and my present-day ongoing love affair with Him, coupled with a growing determination to know Him even more so I can love Him even deeper. I realized that day in the airport that I want to live this faith of mine out loud in a way that's similar to the display of those lovebirds.

I want skeptics to witness my love for Jesus and my desperate desire for more of Him and have their indifferent and hard hearts shaken to the core until they have to begin looking for Him themselves. For the Bible tells us that we can't seek Him without finding Him, and my experience has been that to know Him is to love Him. In the words of that old worship song, "I keep falling in love with Him, over and over, and over and over again." You can, too.

> *More than that, I count all things to be loss in view*
> *of the surpassing value of knowing Christ Jesus my*
> *Lord, for whom I have suffered the loss of all things,*
> *and count them but rubbish so that I may gain Christ.*
> PHILIPPIANS 3:8

SATURDAY

A Hungry Heart Is Sharing

Oh, the advantages of technology. I freely admit to being an avid Facebooker. I'm also LinkedIn, Twitter happy, Pin crazy, and sharing like mad on Instagram. What can I say? I know social media has its detractors, but I believe it is what you make it, and I'm a people person. And yet the development I will talk about today is creepy times two, even for me.

Did you know there is actually a Facebook app that will allow you to post a new status *after* you pass? No, I'm not kidding. It's called the "If I Die" app, and it works like this. You decide on your good-bye message now, while you have the time on your hands, so to speak. Then you choose three "trustees" who must log in and verify your death once you have, well, "logged off" for the last time. Then, and only then, will Facebook post your final message. Granted, you won't know how many people hit "like" or how often your last words get "shared," but if you just can't entertain the idea of being caught speechless, this new technological aid might have your name on it.

The people who created this app say it is the perfect way to leave a final farewell, reveal a long-held secret or—for those who just have to have the last word—a parting insult. If you were to consider such a thing, please bear in mind that your status will be permanent. You can't update it from beyond. They don't have an app for that today, and trust me, they won't be developing one tomorrow.

All joking aside, that would be precisely why we would all do well to remember that we're leaving what could be last-minute messages for our loved ones right now, in this moment. Every day we tell our friends and family and our kids and grandkids what we believe and what we value by what we're saying and what we're doing in real time. They can read our lives and know if we're seeking the kingdom of God or if we're pushing our own agendas.

In a passage in Luke's Gospel, God has something very startling to say on the subject that is clearer than anything I could possibly articulate. To the rich man, God said, "'You fool! This very night your soul is required of you; and now who will own what you have prepared?' So is the man who stores up treasure for himself, and is not rich toward God" (Luke 12:20–21).

Let's be committed to leaving the right message. I've noticed that later usually comes too late.

Yet you do not know what your life will be like tomorrow. You are just a vapor that appears for a little while and then vanishes away.

JAMES 4:14

MONDAY

A Hungry Heart Is Surrendered

My daughter was playing outside with her boys. It was the close of potty training, day two, with the littlest one, and things were going better than she had expected.

"I'm so proud of you," Jessica told Connor. "You're Mama's big boy!"

"Let's tell Keggie," Connor announced. That would be me.

Jessica reached for her phone to call me, but Connor had another plan. Clearly, he'd just decided that if telling Keggie was good, show and tell would be even better. And that is why this Keggie's smartphone buzzed and delivered a picture of Connor with his shorts at his ankles, flashing his Looney Tunes underwear and sporting the cheesiest of grins. Seriously, I'd like nothing more than to share that entire photo with y'all, but we all know I'd get in trouble. You'll have to trust me. The full picture is worth a thousand words. But aren't they all?

As believers, we've often used similar expressions when talking about faith.

"I can't hear what you're saying over what you're doing."

"Your actions speak louder than your words."

And, of course, "Sister, if you're going to talk it, walk it."

And we try, don't we? Oh, how we try—which in and of itself can be the biggest hindrance in discovering the joy of abiding in this Jesus. Stay with me, and I'll explain.

I used to try to will myself to do that or not to say this. Can you say "epic fail"? My friend, there is a more excellent way, and Christ died for us to experience it. For all who can hear and believe, Jesus is God's willpower, so to speak. I have no endless supply of Christian virtues in me, but when I turn to Christ, I have everything I need and more.

As long as we rely on our willpower, we'll never know His. And just as important, if not more, is our witness. For those listening to our talk and comparing it to our walk, a life yielded to Him is truly a picture worth a thousand words.

So that you will walk in a manner worthy of the Lord, to please Him in all respects, bearing fruit in every good work and increasing in the knowledge of God; strengthened with all power, according to His glorious might, for the attaining of all steadfastness and patience; joyously giving thanks to the Father, who has qualified us to share in the inheritance of the saints in Light.

COLOSSIANS 1:10–12

TUESDAY

A Hungry Heart Is Intentional

Life can be hard even when it's good. Can I get a witness?

People adopt various and sundry ways of dealing with daily stress. Some coping mechanisms are healthy, others not so much. Who among us doesn't know someone who is ruining his or her life by trying to calm the madness with fix-me-quick shopping trips or addictive substances like drugs and alcohol?

And those are some of the more destructive things we humans reach for to soothe our souls. There are other coping mechanisms that are just downright strange. I fell down an Internet hole earlier by typing "how people deal with stress" in a search engine. Trust me on this one: you don't even want to know some of the things I discovered quite by accident. In one of the milder examples, a man said that when he feels stressed he starts spelling out what the people around him are saying. That's w-i-e-r-d. I mean, w-e-i-r-d. Thanks, spell check.

By the way, my southern mama insists that cleaning house relieves her stress. I kid you not. As of this writing, that trait has not been passed down to this belle.

My grandchildren have their own ways of handling stress. Their parents have taught them that they can calm themselves by taking a deep breath and letting it out slowly. This isn't my shameless way of mentioning my grandkids again, although that's always fun. Oh, sure, my grands are adorable, taking those deep breaths with tear-streaked faces, but I only mention them because it leads me so seamlessly into my heartfelt recommendation for coping. That would be God's Word. I find the pages of Holy Scripture to be the sweetest and most effective stress reliever on the planet.

The Bible isn't composed of everyday words made from average-Joe letters lined up on a page. Oh no, friend. These words are the very breath of God. And this is where I find my balance. Sure, life is busy and growing increasingly more so, but I've learned the hard way not to let anything steal my time in the Word. It is literally how I breathe. If you have yet to discover the sweet rest of God, allow me to encourage you today to do yourself a huge favor. Determine to take a deep breath of God's Word every single day, and let it out slowly!

But He answered, "It is written: Man must not live on bread alone but on every word that comes from the mouth of God."
MATTHEW 4:4 HCSB

❧ WEDNESDAY ❧

A Hungry Heart Is Praying

Over the last dozen years, I've met numerous wonderful authors, many of whom have kindly shared some of their hard-earned lessons in our industry. I've also been blessed with good counsel from agents and editors, but one of the best pieces of writing advice I've ever received has to be this: "Don't get it right, get it written."

The phrasing makes it easy to remember, but the practice of learning to turn off your inner editor and let the thoughts flow is crucial to getting something down on paper. I've learned that the first words to start lining up seldom make the final cut, and that's okay. It's far more important that I just sit down and start writing, to let myself feel the familiar tap of my fingers on the keyboard as I search for what it is that I really want to say. Once the words start flowing, I can always delete the opening ramble. Granted, some might say my writing style is pretty much a ramble all the way. I would forgive them for that. They don't see what gets trashed!

I've noticed that my prayer times benefit from a similar practice. Maybe it's just me, but sometimes what I start off saying is not at all what I mean. It's stilted and formal and pretty much what I think God wants to hear, but it's not what's on my heart. I can try to pray without opening my mouth and I can try to compose just the right prayer, just the right way. Either approach will just be a meaningless exercise. Nothing life changing happens until I open my mouth and begin to pray. Sometimes I have to come to Him and pour out a bunch of words before I can get to some that matter, but it is so worth it when the fellowship begins to flow.

Maybe this practice could help you discover His sweet friendship. If so, perhaps you could remember it this way: "Don't get it perfect; get it prayed."

Is anyone among you in trouble? Let them pray.
Is anyone happy? Let them sing songs of praise.
JAMES 5:13 NIV

THURSDAY

A Hungry Heart Is Celebrating

For a history buff who enjoys swapping stories with family members and loves worshipping Jesus with like-minded believers, traveling back in time to a small country church where five generations of our clan have worshipped amounts to a red-letter day. The service I describe is an annual event and one I try to attend whenever I can. I was forced to miss the gathering this year, but my heart was with those who made it.

Regular services are no longer held at Hickory Springs, but the small church building constructed in the 1800s far back in the woods of north Louisiana is well kept by loyal descendants of the May family. Once a year friends and family return to those hallowed grounds for a combination reunion and worship service. Present are May family descendants, honorary May family members, and ornery May family members. That last distinction was once offered to me by someone who freely identified himself more with the ornery side.

I filed that funny away with other family tidbits I heard at Hickory Springs for the first time, like those concerning my great-grandfather Harvey's fall from a deer stand at the age of eighty-three. Alone in the woods, unable to get to his feet from the resulting internal injuries, Harvey May summoned the strength to use his rifle like a cane. He even managed to pull himself through a creek bed before help came. I like knowing I come from tough stock.

That said, one of my hands-down fondest memories from these visits is being introduced to people who seemed to love me on sight simply because I am "Ruth's granddaughter and Charlotte's girl." I imagine you've experienced that sort of thing. Meeting someone who loves your people is to enjoy favor that's long been established. You're simply allowed to ride their coattails.

I see in that a beautiful picture of the grace of Christ. As believers, we get to enjoy the favor Father God has for Jesus, His Son. Anyone who desires to know God can come in the name of His Son and be welcomed with open arms. And that is truly a red-letter day!

> *"As the Father has loved me, so have I loved you.*
> *Now remain in my love."*
> JOHN 15:9 NIV

We won't be overcomers
until we are overcome.

A Hungry Heart Is Needy

I have a question for you today, but you may want to hear me out before you raise your hand. *Are you an overcomer?*

I'm pretty sure every believer wants to be. It's one of the promises we like to stand on, isn't it? Finding scripture and verse for such a life is easy enough. One of them is found in 1 John 5:5: "Who is the one who overcomes the world, but he who believes that Jesus is the Son of God?"

By definition, to "overcome" means to endure, to get the better of, to conquer. As believers, we understand that Jesus got the victory over this world and is the Prince of it. And, as hard as it is for us to believe, we gladly accept the truth that His triumph is ours to share. Awesome, right? Yippee skippy! Color us overcomers! Except so many of us aren't.

Ouch.

What we are is needy. And if we are ever to become overcomers, we must understand just how needy we are.

Consider the definitions of the word *overcome*. It means to be seized, grasped, and to have prevailed. Those definitions raise questions for all of us. Have we been overcome by a worship song or a hymn here and there? Have we been taken by a verse from time to time? Or has the Son of God truly overcome us?

We sorely need Jesus to seize our stubborn wills, grasp our "this is my life" mentalities, and prevail over our to-do lists. For we won't be overcomers until we are overcome.

Overcome me, Lord Jesus. Start here.

For whatever is born of God overcomes the world.
And this is the victory that has overcome the world—our faith.
1 JOHN 5:4 NKJV

A Hungry Heart Is Sharing

"Once upon a time. . ." People the world over are enchanted by those words and the power of the story. What story, you might ask? Why, that's easy—any story, every story, and yes, your story. Go ahead. Test it. Begin any presentation or conversation with a simple narrative and see if your audience doesn't immediately engage. Keeping their attention, well, that's another matter, but getting it is as easy as saying, "Let me tell you a story."

The storytelling fascination begins with little kids begging weary parents to read their favorite stories over and over. Then, as time moves on and Curious George and Cinderella lose their appeal, some readers will develop a preference for science fiction. That variety of story will do nothing for those who love the classics. Others may lose themselves in historical romance or any number of different genres, or get their story fix in a different media form entirely, but regardless of their personal predilections, let someone say, "Did you hear about. . . ," and all will tend to pause to see what's coming next.

We southerners like to think we excel in telling stories, and we may have just cause for believing that, but the truth is that love of the story is universal. I think this is by design, that it can be traced to the master storyteller Himself, the One who spoke everything into existence by His words. What if it's no accident that all the world loves a story? What if He set us up?

Think about it. If you're a Christian, those around you are hardwired to listen to your story. Whether in spoken or written form they are primed, so to speak, to hear about your life in Christ.

Don't overthink it. Like all good stories, yours needs a beginning, the day you surrendered your heart to Jesus, but it need not have an incredible outline and a fantastic finish. Actually, it shouldn't be complete at all. It should be an ongoing saga of your experience living this life in submission to and in fellowship with your God.

If you don't have a story, well, that can be fixed, too! See the Father about getting one that's uniquely yours. Oh, in case you're interested, here's the introduction to mine. Once upon a time, I determined to know God, and the more I seek Him, the more I find Him. To be continued. . .

The LORD has looked down from heaven upon the sons of men to see if there are any who understand, who seek after God.

PSALM 14:2

A Hungry Heart Is Surrendered

I remember playing a game called "Mother, May I?" with my cousins and sisters in Natchez, Mississippi. You probably played it yourself growing up, but seeing as it's been a few years for most of us, I'll recap the rules.

In our game everyone lined up together, facing the person who was acting as the lucky first leader, also known as the "Mother." If this person said, "Mother says hop three steps forward while waving your hands," the participants were expected to wave and hop exactly three steps and nothing more. To win, a kid had to pay very close attention. The Mother was always trying to trick some eager soul by giving an instruction without preceding it with those two magic words, "Mother says." If this was the case, you still had to wave and hop exactly three steps but only after you had asked permission—"Mother, may I?"—and received it—"Yes, you may."

If a player moved a muscle before Mother gave permission, said player had to take his or her three steps backward instead. Bummer. The first one to touch the Mother won. May I be perfectly clear? The older kids (namely, Cyndie, Rodney, and Steve) cheated every single time they made it to the leadership position. They didn't want any of us younger kids to win. Hence, they rigged it to make doubly sure we wouldn't get a giant step when we needed one. As you can tell, I've forgiven them long ago. These things are just vague memories.

All joking aside, I'd like to ask you a serious question. Have you ever tried to follow the Lord but felt like you were taking two steps forward and one step back? If so, I'd like to offer you a giant step. For, unlike my sister and her cohorts, your heavenly Father is rooting for you in this game of life. You don't have to have a ton of starts and stops, and He will never trick you by changing the rules! The average believer can take a giant step toward a fulfilling relationship with Jesus by deciding that knowing about Him isn't enough, by determining that he or she must know Him on a personal level to survive and thrive. Oh, and here's the best part: if you want a life-changing relationship with your God, His answer to your fully surrendered "Father, may I?" is always, "Yes, you may."

> *"So let us know, let us press on to know the Lord. His going*
> *forth is as certain as the dawn; and He will come to us*
> *like the rain, like the spring rain watering the earth."*
>
> Hosea 6:3

Putting God's Word in our memory allows the Holy Spirit to bring it back when we need it most.

TUESDAY

A Hungry Heart Is Intentional

I sat spellbound at a conference recently, listening to a brilliant and articulate woman recount tale after intriguing tale of adventurous living in exotic places all over the globe. As far as I could tell, the only place on earth that lady hasn't been is Bull Run Road in Alsatia, Louisiana. Trust me, y'all; she would've stood out like a sore thumb.

Today this woman is a *New York Times* bestselling author. Her novels have been translated into almost every language on the planet and sold millions of copies around the globe. But, as if that weren't impressive enough, she happened to mention that she once wrote computer programs before she started writing bestsellers. Seriously? I was already impressed with her above-average intelligence and remarkable success, but that little bit of bio took the cake. Sure, I've learned to update my website by myself (finally), but I'll never truly understand computers.

For instance, why are computers allowed to hide our files? I remember the first time I was looking for a missing folder and that nice guy at my ISP showed me how to get to the hidden files place. I thought the practice was tacky then, and I still think it's tacky today. I'm always wasting precious time looking for my computer files. The other day I searched my laptop in vain and wasted valuable time that I didn't have looking for a certain document. I finally realized I had saved the blooming thing on my desktop computer. Great. Here's a tip from a not-so-expert source: you can't find it if it isn't there. Brilliant, I know.

Speaking of the importance of recall, here's a tip on a similar but far more valuable subject from John 14:26: "The Helper, the Holy Spirit, whom the Father will send in My name, He will teach you all things, and bring to your remembrance all that I said to you." What a blessed promise of recall assistance that is! And yet as comforting as that verse may be to a believer, it's equally important that we don't miss the obvious implication. We have to do our part and put the Word in us in the first place. If you don't make the effort to put scripture in your memory, there won't be anything for the Holy Spirit to bring back.

Be diligent to present yourself approved to God as
a workman who does not need to be ashamed,
accurately handling the word of truth.
2 TIMOTHY 2:15

Fruit Salad with Poppy Seed Dressing

This fruit salad always makes an appearance at our Fourth of July celebration. It's one of those recipes you'll turn to again and again when the produce aisle is brimming with fresh fruit!

1 pineapple, chopped into bite-size pieces

2 pints fresh strawberries, washed and quartered

1 bunch bananas

4 cups green grapes

1 pint blueberries

1 cup vegetable oil

¼ cup white wine vinegar

½ cup fresh lemon juice (2 to 3 lemons)

½ cup sugar

1½ tablespoons poppy seeds

Mint leaves, for garnish

Prep all your favorite fruits into bite-size pieces. (Peaches aren't listed here, but if you can get your hands on fresh peaches, they absolutely must be included.)

Prepare dressing by whisking vegetable oil with white wine vinegar, lemon juice, and sugar. Season with poppy seeds and stir again.

Transfer prepped fruit into serving bowl. Drizzle with dressing and stir well. If you're not going to serve immediately, store in airtight container to prevent fruit from darkening. Otherwise, dig in! I like to garnish mine with fresh mint leaves.

Cheesy Lasagna with Baby Spinach

Lasagna gets a bad rap for being labor intensive. But it really isn't. It's just a matter of preparing the layers and assembling them. Trust me: your loved ones will agree that it is time well spent.

1 (12 count) package
  lasagna noodles
1 pound bulk sausage
1 pound ground beef
1 teaspoon dried basil
1 teaspoon Italian seasoning
1 teaspoon oregano
1 (24 ounce) can Hunt's
  Garlic & Herb Pasta Sauce
2 (6.5 ounce) cans tomato sauce
2 to 3 tablespoons tomato paste
Salt and pepper

16 ounces ricotta cheese
  (or cottage cheese)
½ cup milk
1 egg
2 tablespoons olive oil
1 tablespoon minced garlic
2 handfuls fresh baby spinach, roughly
  chopped
1 pound fresh mozzarella, shredded
1 cup grated Parmesan cheese
  for topping
Parsley for garnish

Bring lightly salted pot of water to rolling boil. Add lasagna noodles and boil until they begin to soften, about 8 minutes. Drain noodles and rinse with cold water; set aside. Brown sausage and beef. Season with basil, Italian seasoning, and oregano. Drain grease; return meat to skillet. Add pasta sauce, tomato sauce, and tomato paste. Season with salt and pepper and allow to simmer while preparing remaining layers.

For white sauce, combine ricotta cheese with milk and egg. Heat olive oil before adding garlic. Stir in baby spinach; let spinach wilt and cook 2 to 3 minutes before stirring into white sauce.

Spoon half meat sauce in bottom of greased casserole. Layer with half precooked noodles. Spread with half white sauce and spinach, then sprinkle with half shredded mozzarella. Repeat layers. Cover with foil and bake in preheated 350-degree oven for 20 minutes. Remove from oven and top with grated Parmesan. Bake 15 minutes longer. Garnish with parsley before serving.

Layered Strawberry Pecan Delight

Strawberries are abundant in Louisiana come spring, and that suits this family just fine. We can't get enough of them. This recipe uses another of our favorite regional crops—pecans! Just gaze at the butter pecan base in the pic and try not to drool!

CRUST:

2 cups pecans

2 teaspoons butter, melted

3 tablespoons brown sugar

½ teaspoon vanilla

1 tablespoon water

STRAWBERRY LAYER:

1 (6 ounce) package strawberry gelatin

2 cups fresh strawberries, cleaned, sliced, and frozen

CREAM CHEESE LAYER:

1 (8 ounce) package cream cheese, softened

1 cup sugar

1 recipe whipped cream (2 tablespoons powdered sugar, 1 cup heavy cream, 1 teaspoon vanilla), or substitute one 8-ounce carton nondairy whipped topping

Wash and slice strawberries. Freeze overnight. Prepare crust the following day by pulsing pecans in food processor until fine. Add melted butter, brown sugar, vanilla, and water. Pulse again until mixture is crumbly. Press into 9x13 baking dish. Bake in preheated 350-degree oven for 15 to 20 minutes.

Prepare second layer by combining softened cream cheese and sugar. Fold in whipped topping and spread cream cheese mixture over baked and cooled crust. To make whipped cream, add 2 tablespoons powdered sugar to 1 cup heavy cream. Beat in chilled mixing bowl until peaks form, and stir in vanilla. Refrigerate while preparing strawberry topping.

Dissolve strawberry gelatin in two cups boiling water. Add frozen strawberries. Refrigerate gelatin mixture for a few minutes until it becomes syrupy. Don't let it set up! Once it's syrupy, pour over cream cheese layer. Return finished dish to fridge and chill 3 to 4 hours. It's worth the wait, folks. Tomboy honor!

Sensational Asparagus

I took the inspiration for this asparagus dish from my Sensation Salad recipe. You can find that salad in my storytelling cookbook Hungry Is a Mighty Fine Sauce, *but it basically treats your chopped greens with the delicious dressing used here. I simply substituted fresh asparagus on a lark. Score! Win, win! However you describe it, my idea was a hit, even with the non-asparagus people in my family!*

1 pound washed asparagus with woody ends removed

1 cup Romano cheese, grated

¼ cup olive oil

1½ tablespoons concentrated lemon juice, or juice of one lemon

3 teaspoons crushed garlic

Salt and pepper

Place asparagus in single layer on baking sheet and sprinkle with Romano cheese. Whisk olive oil with lemon juice. Stir in crushed garlic. Add salt and pepper to taste. Drizzle asparagus with dressing and bake in preheated 450-degree oven for 12 to 15 minutes. Serve warm and enjoy!

Roasted Avocado and Sesame Oil Hummus from Kitchen Belleicious

I introduced my readers to my food-blogging daughter's website, KitchenBelleicious.com, *in the pages of my storytelling cookbook* Hungry Is a Mighty Fine Sauce. *Here's another of Jessica's dishes. She developed this Roasted Avocado and Sesame Oil Hummus for her gluten-free readers.*

1 large avocado

⅛ cup olive oil, or more, depending on desired consistency

½ teaspoon each salt and pepper

1 can chickpeas, drained

1 teaspoon toasted sesame seed oil

1 lime, juiced

½ teaspoon garlic powder

Prepare avocado by peeling it, cutting it into quarters, and discarding stone. Drizzle with tablespoon of olive oil; season with salt and pepper. Bake in preheated 400-degree oven for 15 minutes. Remove and allow to cool.

Drain chickpeas and pulse in food processor with toasted sesame seed oil and remaining olive oil. Add lime juice and garlic powder. Pulse a few more times and add cooled avocado. Pulse again, adding a little more olive oil if necessary until hummus is smooth. Taste and add more salt and pepper if desired. Serve with your favorite chip or cracker—gluten-free if you need to—and enjoy!

Shellie's Go-To Boston Butt Recipe

I have an often used and much loved barbecue pulled pork recipe in my tried-and-true file. This, however, is the supereasy pulled pork method I use when I don't want a barbecue taste. It produces tons of flavor and a delightful sauce from its own juices. Serve it as a great main meat dish for a dinner and then use the leftovers in a dish like my Pulled Pork Corn Chowder, featured on the following page.

1 Boston butt
Your favorite pork rub
   (mine is pepper, Cajun seasoning,
   and paprika)

1 large white onion, sliced
2 to 3 garlic cloves, diced

Rub Boston butt with your favorite pork seasonings. Don't be too cautious here. Season it well, maybe a tablespoon or so of each! Set aside to rest.

Place sliced onion in slow cooker. Layer diced garlic over onions. You're almost done. Seriously! Simply place pork butt on onion and garlic bed, place lid on slow cooker, and step away for 8 to 10 hours while pork cooks on low. (I like to sear mine first on all sides in my heavy cast-iron skillet, but you don't have to if you're short on time. One of the benefits of doing so, however, is that gorgeous look of the fully cooked rubbed roast in the photo!)

This pork butt will make a delicious sauce all on its own. Of course, if you're using it for pulled pork sandwiches, you may want to add barbecue sauce as a condiment.

The Belle's Pulled Pork Corn and Potato Chowder

This chowder utilizes the leftover pork from my Boston Butt recipe on the previous page. Making one dish pull double duty is a great way to feed your loved ones and lighten a busy schedule at the same time.

3 to 4 large potatoes, diced
1 stick butter
1 (10 ounce) bag frozen vegetable blend (onion, celery, bell pepper)
1 garlic clove, minced
½ cup flour, divided
4 cups pulled pork stock
2 cups half-and-half

1 cup chicken stock
1 cup water
1 (16 ounce) bag frozen corn
Salt and pepper, to taste
Pinch nutmeg, freshly ground
Green onions, sliced
Cheddar cheese, grated

Wash, peel, and prep spuds into bite-size pieces. Melt butter in skillet and sauté diced onion, celery, and bell pepper. Once veggies are tender and clear, add garlic.

Time to make a roux. Remove veggies with slotted spoon and transfer them to your slow cooker (or soup pot if you're cooking on stovetop). Gradually stir 2 to 3 tablespoons of flour into remaining butter. Stir until roux turns light brown. Add 4 cups of stock reserved from cooking Boston butt, along with two cups half-and-half and 1 cup each of chicken stock and water. Add liquids slowly to avoid clumps. Transfer this stock to slow cooker, set heat to low, and your chowder is off to a delicious start.

Add parboiled potatoes and frozen corn. (Parboil just means to add them to a pot of boiling water until they begin to get tender.) Stir well, season with salt and pepper and a pinch of nutmeg, and allow to cook on low for 4 to 6 hours so flavors can blend. *Yum!* Top chowder with green onions and a bit of grated cheddar cheese.

Sweet Potato Swirl

My Sweet Potato Swirl has officially converted more than a few anti–sweet potato folks—yours truly included. As a bonus, it makes a beautiful presentation. And that gives it extra marks in my book!

½ pound bacon
5 sweet potatoes
1 cup butter, melted

3 tablespoons brown sugar
1 tablespoon cinnamon
Salt and pepper, to taste

Fry bacon in a cast-iron skillet. Remove bacon and save the grease. Cool bacon, crumble, and set aside. Slice washed and peeled sweet potatoes into thinnest slices possible. (Shhh—that's a tricky step that makes these babies more appealing to folks who think they aren't sweet potato fans!) Combine melted butter, brown sugar, and cinnamon in mixing bowl. Add sweet potato slices and toss well.

Using skillet that still contains bacon grease, construct swirl by propping slices against sides of the skillet one by one, overlapping edges. Once outside circle is complete, start another, and repeat until you have a gorgeous swirl of sweet potatoes that ends in a tight curl in middle of skillet. Perfect!

Sprinkle with crumbled bacon and salt and pepper to taste, and bake in preheated 350-degree oven for about an hour, or until potatoes are fork tender.

Mama's Hot Fried Corn Bread

Some recipes have a way of falling off your radar. It happened to me with Mama's Hot Fried Corn Bread (also known as hoecakes)—that is, until I popped in on my parents one day just in time to see Mama dropping these sweet darlings into a hot skillet. Have mercy. Please don't ask me how many servings I had that day or how many times I've prepared these since. I need to keep some things to myself. Don't take this recipe lightly, y'all. It's got flavor, plus.

1 (8.5 ounce) box Jiffy
    corn muffin mix
1 to 2 tablespoons self-rising flour
1 egg
¾ cup buttermilk to make a
    thick consistency
2 to 3 heaping tablespoons
    cornmeal mix
¼ to ½ cup vegetable oil
Salt

Mama doesn't bother with a scratch mix for these little beauties, although she could if she wanted. No, for her fried corn bread, she starts with a box of Jiffy corn muffin mix. Prepare with one egg per package directions but use buttermilk instead of whole milk and a bit of extra cornmeal mix. That's to help the little darlings stick together better for frying.

Per Mama's instructions, cover bottom of skillet with vegetable oil. We're not deep frying, y'all. This is what southerners call "quick frying." When oil is hot, drop corn bread in by teaspoons. Let it fry on one side till it begins to brown. Flip it over and flatten it with spatula or spoon. This allows it to fry all the way through without being in the grease too long. Once it's brown on both sides, drain on paper towels, salt lightly, and enjoy!

Grandma Stone's Butter Pecan Muffins

Grandma Stone's Butter Pecan Muffins aren't supersweet, which makes them perfectly suited for breakfast. (Or snack, or supper, or. . . you get me?)

¼ cup butter, melted and cooled
1½ cups flour
2¼ teaspoons baking powder
½ teaspoon salt
1 cup chopped pecans

½ cup brown sugar, firmly packed
1 egg, well beaten
¾ cup milk
1 teaspoon vanilla

Preheat oven to 400 degrees and melt ¼ cup butter. Set butter aside to cool. Line muffin tin with 10 cupcake liners. (Tip: Put a tablespoon or so of water in the remaining two tins and your muffins will bake evenly.)

Prepare dry ingredients by combining flour with baking powder and salt. Whisk in chopped pecans and brown sugar.

In separate bowl, combine well-beaten egg with cooled butter, milk, and vanilla. Combine liquid ingredients with dry ones and stir just until dry ingredients are incorporated. (Warning: Stirring too much will give you packy muffins. Nobody wants that.) Divide batter between liners and bake for about 15 minutes. Remove them when they're golden brown and they spring back to a light touch.

Shellie's Deep-Dish Skillet Pizza

It all began with a burst of kitchen inspiration. I was wondering how or if it was possible to create a deep-dish pizzeria-worthy crust from plain old refrigerator pizza dough when the answer hit me like a ton of bricks—or at least like a heavy skillet. Why not my cast-iron skillet? I mean, why not? Why haven't I thought of this before? I had no idea, but the result was very satisfying. My Deep-Dish Skillet Pizza will make you think you're sitting at your favorite pizza restaurant.

2 tablespoons olive oil

2 (14.5 ounce) cans Hunt's Basil, Garlic & Oregano tomato sauce

2 tablespoons tomato paste

3 to 4 tablespoons grated three-cheese blend of Romano, Asiago, and Parmesan

¾ teaspoon dried oregano, crushed

¾ teaspoon dried basil, crushed

½ teaspoon crushed red pepper

2 (13.8 ounce) cans Pillsbury refrigerated pizza dough

8 ounces Italian bulk sausage, browned and drained

½ pound ground beef, browned and drained

½ package pepperoni slices

2 cups shredded mozzarella

Preheat oven to 475 degrees. Brush bottom of cast-iron skillet with olive oil. (FYI: For these ingredients I used my 16-inch skillet. If you use a smaller skillet, you may want to scale back.) Prepare pizza sauce by combining tomato sauce, tomato paste, and three-cheese blend. Season with crushed oregano, basil, and red pepper. Set aside.

Combine two cans refrigerated pizza dough into one ball. Lay dough on floured surface and roll into a circle a bit larger than the bottom of your cast-iron skillet. Place circle of dough in skillet and pinch extra dough around edges to create a rolled crust and a well for your sauce and fixings. Top dough with sauce and meats of your choice. Top with shredded mozzarella and bake for 15 to 20 minutes, or until your crust is browned to your personal preference.

Summer's Garden Fresh Pasta

Sautéed spinach and baby tomatoes pair with Kalamata olives and a couple different cheeses in my Garden Fresh Pasta to deliver big flavor. You can stir it up and serve it right away, but it gets even better if you chill it overnight.

12 ounces of your favorite pasta
1 cup chicken broth
10 ounces fresh spinach
½ bunch green onions
1 (9.5 ounce) jar Kalamata olives
2 to 3 tablespoons olive oil

3 to 4 garlic cloves, minced
10 ounces baby plum tomatoes, halved
Coarse salt and black pepper
½ cup Parmesan cheese, grated
2 to 3 tablespoons Italian dressing
½ cup feta cheese

Cook pasta per package instructions in boiling water along with a cup of chicken broth. Drain and place in serving bowl.

Wash fresh spinach and give it a rough chop. Dice green onions and Kalamata olives.

Heat olive oil in cast-iron skillet. Add half minced garlic. Sauté briefly, maybe a minute, just to let garlic infuse the oil—but don't let it burn. Add spinach and stir until it wilts before transferring it with a slotted spoon to serving bowl with pasta. (FYI: Y'all, you don't have to sauté the spinach, but I think doing so delivers more flavor throughout the dish.) Add another tablespoon of oil to pan along with remaining garlic, stir a few seconds, and add baby tomatoes. Season with salt and black pepper and cook for a few minutes until tomatoes start puckering.

Add tomatoes to serving bowl with drained pasta and spinach. Stir in olives, green onions, Parmesan cheese, and just enough bottled Italian dressing to wet the dish— 2 to 3 tablespoons should do it. Top with feta cheese prior to serving.

WEDNESDAY

A Hungry Heart Is Praying

When I was a little girl growing up on Bull Run Road, late summer and early fall evenings seemed to go on forever. I remember catching magical fireflies in mason jars and playing hide-and-seek as the mosquitoes feasted on our bare legs. In the midst of the game, their bites were nothing more than a minor distraction. We unconsciously splattered them against our skin in the fading dark as we tended to weightier matters like whose turn was it to be "it" first. (Since I was the baby of the family, it was usually mine.) Only later, lying beneath the cool sheets, having been forced through baths and examined by eagle-eyed Mama, would we realize the extent of the mosquito attacks. How in the world did Mama expect us not to scratch? Seriously, I didn't understand it then and I still don't today.

But, back to hide-and-seek. . . As I alluded to earlier, being the youngest meant I had considerably more practice being the seeker than the hider. Always the optimist, I'd search diligently for my older sisters, fully trusting that they were going to let me take my turn hiding sooner or later. Whether it was due to the fading dark or the large boundaries of the surrounding fields, more often than I care to remember, I had to swallow my pride and call out the admission that shames little children everywhere: "I give up. Come out, come out, wherever you are!"

Those long-ago memories of hide-and-seek remind me of a beautiful promise from God's Word. The Bible teaches us that apart from His revelation, there is no searching out God. Wow, that makes for one futile game of hide-and-seek, and it means that however smart, however educated one may be, God won't allow Himself to be known by the casual observer. He will remain a mystery. But don't despair! As the late Paul Harvey would say, here's the rest of the story!

The same Good Book also tells us in Jeremiah 29:13 that God will be found of those who search for Him with all of their hearts. I urge you to find yourself a quiet place that you can return to over and over again, a place to renew your mind and your strength, a place where you can lift your voice in earnest to the One who desires to be found. Approach Him like a small child willing to risk your reputation to call, "Come out, come out, wherever you are," and you'll come to know your Maker.

Hast thou not known? hast thou not heard, that the everlasting God, the LORD, the Creator of the ends of the earth, fainteth not, neither is weary? there is no searching of his understanding.
ISAIAH 40:28 KJV

THURSDAY

A Hungry Heart Is Celebrating

I doubt any of you could have seen the faded marks on my chest if I didn't point them out, but I could see them for a long time because I knew where to look, and I looked quite often. They're completely gone now, but I've held on to the lesson they taught me. I called those leftover marks my "love wounds." They were gifts from my youngest grandchild.

Connor Maher once had a habit of playing with our skin while we were holding him close. He wasn't trying to hurt us. It wasn't like he pinched on purpose. He just liked to, well, fiddle with our skin. Connor was nineteen months old at the time, and he had no idea that his baby fingernails were leaving scratches.

As strange as this is going to sound, it was always kind of sad for me to watch those marks begin to fade. Connor lives in Texas with his parents and his older brother, Grant Thomas. It doesn't matter how often I burn up the roads from Lake Providence to Houston, this grandmother doesn't get to see those boys as often as she would like. I miss them, all of them. Watching the marks on my chest fade was a sweet reminder of our visits. They also kept me anticipating the next time I'd get to those grand beau czars of Texas. In short, the scars were special because of the one who left them there.

Does that not remind you of another set of love wounds? Someone else with scars in His hands and His feet, with injuries to His brow, His back, and His side? It's been two thousand plus years since our sins marred the body of Jesus Christ, and praise God, those love wounds haven't faded.

The Holy Scriptures tell us that one day all believers will look upon that blessed body that was pierced for us, and what a glorious day that will be. But let us revel, for now, in this blessed thought: today, when Jesus looks at those scars of His that will never fade, He sees those He died to save. His wounds are special because of those who left them there. It's okay if you need to shout. I have and I will. Praise the Lamb of God who gladly bears the scars of our redemption!

> *Then He said to Thomas, "Reach here with your finger,*
> *and see My hands; and reach here your hand and put it*
> *into My side; and do not be unbelieving, but believing."*
> JOHN 20:27

FRIDAY

A Hungry Heart Is Needy

Hundreds of years ago, a French philosopher named René Descartes shut himself up in a room to do some thinking. He did a lot of thinking, too. In fact, good old René did so much thinking that even today people are still thinking about one of the things he thought. René's the fellow who said: "I think, therefore I am."

I don't know how René got his most important thought to go viral, as this was centuries before Al Gore invented the Internet; but word got around, and René's big thought has been cussed and discussed ever since. From what I understand, René was saying that the very ability to think proves that the one who is doing the thinking exists.

I'll be honest. I could think about René's big thought all day long, and I still wouldn't see why it's such a big revelation; but then I'm no philosopher. I'm simply a Jesus-loving, story-stacking country girl who is about to say something that will sound unbelievably audacious to the intellectuals among us. Bear with me, brilliant people, but I would like to suggest that René's sentence stops a mite short.

How about "I think, therefore I am angry" or "I think, therefore I am sad, or worried, or —." (You fill in the blank.) All I'm saying is that our thoughts may very well prove our existence, but they also dictate our experience.

It's precisely why you'll find me telling the Lord these days that I simply can't be trusted to be alone with my thoughts. I've come to understand that I need Him in all of them. What's more, I want Him in all of them because apart from Him, my thoughts can deteriorate quickly. This after so many early years in the faith when my attitude was that if I had given God a dutiful block of my attention, the rest of the day and all of my thinking was mine. I sense God's pleasure that I finally understand just how needy I am. I realize my big thought won't draw anywhere near the attention René's did, but here's my conclusion: I think, therefore I need God in all of my thoughts. So do you. Think about it.

For as he thinks within himself, so he is.

PROVERBS 23:7

SATURDAY

A Hungry Heart Is Sharing

Recently I awoke in the middle of the night, vaguely aware of a sensation I couldn't quite place but couldn't shake either, knowing only that it felt familiar in a déjà vu sort of way. Seconds later my retrospection was replaced by an urgent call to action. I hurried to the bathroom and grabbed a tissue, just in the nick of time. And there I sat, four decades past some of the most embarrassing memories of my childhood, employing all the old tricks I once knew so well to try to stop my nose from bleeding. *What in the world?* I could no more imagine where this nighttime nosebleed had come from than I could stop the flood of memories and long-buried emotions.

Time and again in my early childhood, I was forced to hit pause and sit on the sidelines of whatever activity I'd been engaged in because my nose had started bleeding yet again, without warning, and without any apparent cause. I remember the doctors telling my parents not to worry. They were sure it was something I'd outgrow. Thanks, Doc. I thought that was pretty self-serving seeing as he wasn't the one being ridiculed every time it happened. "Ugh! Shellie's nose is bleeding again," my classmates would taunt if it happened at school. "Can you go somewhere else and do that?"

my older sisters would say if it happened at home. The message was clear. Blood may be a necessary reality, but it's definitely not socially appealing.

The other night as I sat there reliving that childhood angst, I thought about how often I sense a similar unease from people about the blood of Jesus and the mighty work of the cross. For the most part, God is a generally acceptable name to drop in almost any conversation, especially here in the Bible Belt. But mention Jesus Christ and the blood of the Lamb, and you'll be taking the risk of upsetting the balance of many a public discourse. Indeed, things can get messy quickly when blood is involved. It's something this country girl knows full well; and yet because it is the very blood of Jesus Christ that cleanses us from sin, redeems us to God, and offers all comers abundant life now and eternal life later, we shouldn't stop proclaiming it. And I won't even try.

*But now in Christ Jesus you who formerly were far
off have been brought near by the blood of Christ.*
Ephesians 2:13

MONDAY

A Hungry Heart Is Surrendered

"Sticks and stones might break my bones, but words will never hurt me!" Wrong. As adults, we've long since figured out that the childhood nursery rhyme we sang to protect ourselves couldn't be further from the truth. We no longer deny that words can be mighty painful. What both fascinates and challenges me is their power to change the world.

Picture if you will, the disciples of Christ sitting in an upper room waiting and praying, praying and waiting. Before leaving in the clouds, Jesus had promised to send them power to take His message to the ends of the earth. He didn't tell them what this power would look like or how long they'd have to wait for it, only that they must.

Finally, after days and nights of waiting, after all the anticipation and questions surrounding this mysterious force Jesus had spoken of, after weeks of wondering what this supernatural aid might be and how they would wield it, God's promise fell as "tongues as of fire" (Acts 2:3).

How strange. Fiery cloven tongues of an otherworldly origin.

I find it fascinating that out of all the body parts the writer could've used to describe this amazing scene when God's fire power fell on humans, He chose the tongue. What a visual of God's plan to employ these fleshy instruments of ours to speak from the understanding of one human to that of another, each witnessing of the consuming fire lit in his or her heart.

That said, is it any wonder that we're so strictly charged to monitor our tongues and the power of language? How can it be that we allow ourselves to use whatever words we want with whomever we want whenever we want—knowing God has chosen these same tongues as holy messengers to take His Gospel into all the world?

May our tongues have fire power because they're yielded to His will instead of our whim.

Let the words of my mouth and the meditation of my heart be
acceptable in your sight, O LORD, my rock and my redeemer.
PSALM 19:14 ESV

TUESDAY

A Hungry Heart Is Intentional

When I was a little girl growing up on Bull Run Road, I was occasionally attacked by overzealous relatives and old friends of my parents. "Look at you. Why, you were just knee high to a grasshopper last time I saw you, girl. Come over here and give Great Aunt Liz a big ole hug and kiss." I remember wanting to escape, but Mama would be looking at me through narrowed eyes. It didn't take a child genius to translate that message, "and act like you like it—or else." I knew I was supposed to act as tickled to see these people as they were to see me, but it was hard when I didn't know the visitor from Adam.

Raise your hand if you can relate. At some point in your childhood, someone expected you to respond to an exuberant relative, but you just weren't feeling the love. Chances are it was because you simply had not spent time with them. Hence, you didn't know them.

A simple analogy can be drawn between that childhood experience and our average church worship service. Many a song leader, preacher, pastor, or visiting speaker has tried to stir up the hearts of the congregation to respond in love to a loving Father. But sometimes, maybe even oftentimes, their listeners don't know the One they're asked to adore.

It's entirely possible to be born again into the family of God by salvation and not come to love Him, truly love Him, because we refuse to spend time with Him. The book of Romans calls our Father "Abba." The closest translation in our language would be Daddy. That's a term of affection, but it's a foreign concept to the one who doesn't feel the affection.

Here's a promise, and it's backed by God's Word. If we'll set ourselves to know Him and begin a quest to understand Him through His love letter, the Bible, we'll fall in love with Him and our response to Him in worship will be genuine and fulfilling.

Simply put, we won't worship Him lavishly if we know Him casually.

So that Christ may dwell in your hearts through faith;
and that you, being rooted and grounded in love, may be able to
comprehend with all the saints what is the breadth and length and
height and depth, and to know the love of Christ which surpasses
knowledge, that you may be filled up to all the fullness of God.

EPHESIANS 3:17–19

❧ WEDNESDAY ❧

A Hungry Heart Is Praying

For as long as I can remember, people have been telling me to "get still." When I was a kid, if I wasn't wiggling too much in church, I was squirming too much in class. It was true then, and it's true now. I fidget. I was about to say "sue me," but I stopped myself. Someone might decide to take me up on it, and who knows where that could go? We've all seen those strange but true verdicts, like the $500,000 a Pennsylvania jury instructed a pair of homeowners to pay a man who broke into their home. From what I can understand, the intruder sued them for mental anguish when their faulty garage door prevented him from exiting their premises. Bless his heart. He had to survive for days on Diet Pepsi and dog food. Never you mind that he was trying to flee the garage after robbing the couple's home. That's just details right there. Besides, I can't tell y'all about that story because we're talking about fidgeting.

As the saying goes, if I had a dollar for every time someone asked me to "get still," I'd be a rich woman. That's not to say that everyone asked. Some of 'em threatened. I'm looking at you, Mama. You, too, Papa.

Bless my darling husband's heart, he's not a fan of the incessant motion either, but he's learned to abide by all my fidgeting. For the most part. That's okay. I'm not a fan of the "be still" request, for the most part. I do, however, have one exceptional exception.

I've learned to relish God's words from Psalm 46:10, "Be still, and know that I am God" (NIV).

The discipline of prayer has become life to me. And don't let anyone ever tell you that a healthy prayer life doesn't begin as a discipline. I would beg to disagree, but that's another devotion for another day.

Learning to be still before God yields immeasurable rewards. I've grown to love placing myself before Him first thing every morning. Does it take me a little time to quit wiggling, quiet my thoughts, and settle in before Him? Absolutely. But nothing compares to starting a day with the One who made it. If you don't have this soul-fortifying, comforting practice, there's only one thing left for me to say: "Be still."

LORD, in the morning you will hear my voice; in the morning
I will pray to you, and I will watch for your answer.

PSALM 5:3 ISV

*God's delight in His ongoing work
in us stems from His joy in the
finished work of Christ for us.*

A Hungry Heart Is Celebrating

Heads up, all you do-it-yourselfers and HGTV fans. Before y'all commit to any size home remodeling project, it would behoove you to refresh yourselves on the three stages of any home improvement plan. I refer to them as: "Let's do it!" "Why are we doing it?" and "We did it!"

My man and I have just finished making over our master bedroom and bathroom, so this is fresh experience speaking. For a while it seemed we might never get out of stage two. It was hard enough to remember why we were doing it when mortar dust started blanketing everything in sight, despite the sheets of plastic that were supposed to contain it to one room, but our enthusiasm took a direct hit the day the water pipe was accidentally busted. You don't get this type of information from Algebra I, but trust me, water plus mortar equals mud—concrete mud.

To make it ever more fun, it happened that I was also meeting myself coming and going to various speaking engagements during those long weeks of remodeling. This means Beloved Hubby and our contractor, who had now become one of the family, were asking me questions over the phone that were way above my pay grade. (That's okay. I may have asked Mr. Contractor his opinion a couple times during it all, too. "Hey Ronnie, should I wear the black boots with this outfit or the brown?")

Glory hallelujah, stage three finally arrived. We did it! Stage two may have been ugly, but when we survey the finished project today we are very pleased with what we see. As believers, you and I are kind of like stage two. We're works in progress, amen? It's why I take great comfort from Philippians 1:6, "I am confident of this very thing, that He who began a good work in you will perfect it until the day of Christ Jesus."

But can I tell you what truly astounds me? It's knowing that even as Jesus is completing the good work He has begun in us, His Father and ours is already pleased with what He sees in us, and it's all because of Jesus.

I know! It's crazy good, but let us celebrate the amazing truth that God looks upon us with pleasure because He sees the finished work of Christ. I can almost hear the two of them now, surveying the work of the cross and announcing with joy, "We did it!"

His pleasure is not in the strength of the horse, nor his delight in the legs of the warrior; the LORD delights in those who fear him, who put their hope in his unfailing love.

PSALM 147:10–11 NIV

FRIDAY

A Hungry Heart Is Needy

I hesitate to broach the following conversation because every time I mention how much I dislike spiders, my Facebook wall gets flooded with images of the little monsters, compliments of people who call themselves my friends. And yet they enjoy harassing me. What is that?

You'd think I'd skirt the subject entirely, and I would—if Father God would keep His spiders out of the state of Louisiana, out of my house, and out of my kayak. What? I don't think that's too much to ask. I've had to knowingly share more than a few of my early morning kayak rides with one of His spiders because the evil things decided to come out of hiding a great distance from a dock and my remaining option was to bail. Not that I haven't considered that, because some of His Louisiana spiders are the size of a small purse dog. You're rolling your eyes, aren't you?

My man does that about my spider thing, too. That hard-working farmer of mine could retire if he had a dollar for every time I've hollered at him from another room because I've spotted a spider and it's trying to get me.

"It's not trying to get you," Phil the Incredibly Patient One says. *Whatever.*

Listen, y'all. I admit I could use perspective on God's spiders, but I'll also freely confess right here that I need tons of perspective, period. All the time. About everything. If you'll forgive me for being blunt, so do you.

This perpetual need of perspective is one of the countless blessings I've found of keeping my eyes trained on Jesus. Here's the simplest way I know to say it. We're constantly presented with two options. When our eyes aren't on Jesus, self is in charge by default. And, oh boy, then we're looking at things through our own skewed lens, which can lead to all sorts of problems.

I know my "self" can turn a careless comment into an accusation and sometimes into always. When my eyes are on me, I can feel unappreciated and misunderstood, or worse. Just being honest. "There is a way that appears to be right, but in the end it leads to death" (Proverbs 14:12 NIV).

On the other hand, when my eyes are on God, I can experience the joy of knowing I'm loved and understood by my good, good Father. Where do you go for perspective?

All the ways of a man are clean in his own sight,
but the LORD weighs the motives.

PROVERBS 16:2

147

SATURDAY

A Hungry Heart Is Sharing

Yesterday my doctor told me he wanted to do a CT scan of my brain. This came as no surprise to the family jokers around here, but it isn't the functions of my strange brain that are concerning the man, y'all. Doc is worried about my recurring ear infections and the possible damage to my hearing if they persist. Seeing the poor man wave his hands in despair after he peeked in my ears and throat, and watching him gesture dramatically toward the bright red hazardous waste box to indicate the color he was seeing was enough to get my full cooperation. So, yes, I'll be making those follow-up appointments his nurse scheduled with the various experts. My ears hurt. I'll take help wherever I can find it. I'm human that way, aren't you?

Two shots, four prescriptions, and twenty-four hours later, I'm not quite up to yippee skippy, but the flesh is getting better and the spirit is mighty thankful. I'm grateful for the wisdom God has given to those in the medical profession. Heck, I want to hug the whole family practice clinic staff for whatever part they played in yesterday's visit. But, more than that, I want to invite you to share with me a greater truth.

If it hurts us directly, we want out. If it's the suffering of others, we're tempted to avert our eyes, wondering how we can really make a difference. And yet God saw misery and pain and devised a way to get right smack in the middle of it through His beloved Son and our Savior, Jesus Christ—and we're called to imitate Him! Here's what I'm learning. Suffering abounds. We can't meet everyone's needs, but we all can do something; and the more involved we become in the needy world around us, we're less tempted to flip the channel or avert our gaze. The next time someone asks us to give to alleviate someone's suffering, instead of thinking of all the others we can't help, let's concentrate on those we can. Like the example set by our sweet Jesus, let's become those people who see pain and find a way to get in it.

So then, while we have opportunity, let us do good to all people,
and especially to those who are of the household of the faith.
GALATIANS 6:10

A Hungry Heart Is Surrendered

It was early morning and I was pumping arm weights while going through my treadmill routine. I'd progressed through the warm-up walk and onto the jogging sequence on the built-in software's interval training when I realized that I had left my water bottle out of reach on the bedside table. *Drat!*

Convinced I was dying of thirst and that I must have water pronto lest I perish, I attempted to get off the treadmill without pulling the kill switch cord and interrupting my workout.

Feeling quite perky, I concluded that surely I could step off the moving track and onto the stationary frame without falling. That would let me reach for my water on the dresser next to my treadmill and get right back to jogging without losing my recorded progress. (Being goal oriented has its drawbacks.) I suppose it could have been a good idea, only I placed my left foot on the stationary frame to the left of the moving belt without immediately following suit with my right foot. I was going to, mind you, had I not started falling faster than quick.

Interestingly, even as I was falling, banging up my shin, and reaching for the kill switch, and recovering and falling and banging up my knee, I remember being incredulous at the injustice of what was happening. For goodness' sake, I'd already determined to get off the blame thing, and yet here I was taking a licking anyway.

And that brings us to the takeaway I'm hoping to secure deep down in our souls. Turning to Jesus requires turning away from our status quo. We simply can't keep one foot in the fallen things of this world, whether it's actions or thought patterns—and expect to live in the grace-filled embrace of Christ. Anything less than severing from the old life will allow it to continue beating the daylights out of us while we bemoan the injustice of it all because, for goodness' sake, we've changed already!

To embrace the present with Jesus, we must hit the kill switch to our past.

Draw near to God and He will draw near to you.
Cleanse your hands, you sinners; and purify
your hearts, you double-minded.

JAMES 4:8

TUESDAY

A Hungry Heart Is Intentional

I walked down the long hall of my home and pushed open the bedroom door with a grateful heart. I'd been looking forward to this moment for hours. It had been a very long day, and I was more than ready to shut down everything for the night. I remember thinking to myself, *So this is what middle age looks like—when you look forward to going to sleep with the type of anticipation you once reserved for a big social event.*

About that time, a noise startled my train of thought. It took a moment for me to identify the repetitive taps on the picture window beside my bed as the water sprinkler. *Great!* I'd left the sprinkler running on the flower bed, which now felt like a million miles away. I considered waiting for Phil to get out of the shower and asking him to go turn it off. He's the man who left for the farm before 6:00 a.m., came home at 9:30 p.m., and drove a combine in the interim. Nah, that would be flat-out wrong. I should do it myself.

I stepped into my trusty garden shoes and slipped out the back door toward the far corner of the house, immediately regretting my lazy decision not to grab a flashlight. I'd counted on using the light from the bathroom window to turn off the faucet. It would work, too, except that I'd have to walk in darkness until I got there. *Nice going, genius.* I scolded myself. Where was the moon when you needed it? By the time I made it back inside, I'd been spooked and scratched by the devilish grasping fingers of an overhead tree limb and maimed by a sunken hole in our bone-dry backyard. I'd like to think I was a little bit wiser, too, but the jury's still out.

I fell asleep thinking about a serious parallel to my nighttime experience. Christians routinely make a far greater mistake than I made by not grabbing a flashlight when they neglect to pick up God's Word. The Bible can't be a lamp to our feet and a light to our path if it's gathering dust on the nightstand. While neglecting God's Word is a mistake that brings much more serious consequences than the ones I suffered in my backyard, the good news is that I had an opportunity early on to stop and go back for the light. So do you.

O send out Your light and Your truth, let them lead me;
let them bring me to Your holy hill and to Your dwelling places.

PSALM 43:3

❧ WEDNESDAY ❧

A Hungry Heart Is Praying

Experts in the study of alien cultures not only believe in their existence, but these authorities are convinced that these other worldly citizens are eavesdropping on our radio broadcasts. When I consider some of the tongue-tangling mistakes I've made on live radio, that idea alone becomes intriguing on a number of levels, but it gets better. They say planet Earth's earliest radio broadcasts are now some eighty light-years away, and it is most likely these radio waves that the extraterrestrials are tuning into as they prepare to contact us.

If I may quote the dog from the Jetsons, that space-age family of my childhood, "Ruh-roh!" This would mean that the curious aliens are forming impressions of us based on songs like "Yes, We Have No Bananas." Boy, are they in for a few surprises when they get to planet Earth. The airwaves aren't carrying many songs about bananas these days, but they are definitely sporting a goodly number of fruits and nuts.

I'm having some fun here, but it's just that I'm not so sure André the Alien is out there listening to the sounds radiating from our world and rocking to "By the Light of the Silvery Moon." On the other hand, I am very convinced of the reality of Someone who is looking on us, and the Bible tells me He is not far from any of us. When I look around me at the wonder of this creation, it's easy to cast my faith in its Creator; and according to Revelation 5:8, God isn't listening to show tunes, but rather to the prayers of His people. The Bible even says He collects those prayers in bowls (Revelation 5:8)!

Someone might ask, "But Shellie, why does He collect so many prayers and seem to answer so few?" Fair question. I don't have all the answers, but I will venture to offer a simple theory from a simple-minded believer. Perhaps it's because so many are self-centered and so few line up with His will, for here's a wonderful secret: when we get the focus off ourselves and begin to pray His will and His Word for our friends and relatives, He shows up and shows off.

Unlike the Martians who may be bumping to the generational beat of our great-great-grandparents, God is relative today. He saw and heard our very first sounds—and any prayer we may have formed since. He knows where you were yesterday, where you are today, and what His plans are for you tomorrow. Our goal should be to get on His wavelength and watch Him come through loud and clear.

Your eyes have seen my unformed substance;
and in Your book were all written the days that were
ordained for me, when as yet there was not one of them.

PSALM 139:16

A Hungry Heart Is Celebrating

My author friends and I agree, it's best not to go there. "There" would be the online review sites where anybody capable of operating a keyboard is free to opine on our books. The challenge is that our publishers and agents also tell us how important those reviews are in helping to spread our message. And that's how it is that a belle who passionately believes in the message of her latest book and wants to share it far and wide can wander over to those sites, despite her better judgment, and get waylaid if she stays too long.

See, I can generally find enthusiastic reviews, and sometimes I can even find less-than-enthusiastic reviews that still manage to be quite helpful. But stay long enough and it's a given: I'm going to get overwhelmed by the ugly. People have ugly to spare. I'm reminded of the old saying, some folks find fault like there's a reward for it.

Nothing good ever comes out of giving too much time or too much weight to people's opinions, including our own. And that brings me right back to my life's message. I talk a lot about this, and I'll continue to share it as long as God gives me breath: introspection is the enemy of anyone who wants to grow closer to Jesus.

Just as our salvation is in Christ Jesus, so is our spiritual growth. We must think less of us and more of Him. Jesus is not some resource hidden under the muck of the believer's heart. He is a person, the God-man who rescued us. When we worship Him, He transforms us.

> *But we all, with unveiled face, beholding*
> *as in a mirror the glory of the Lord,*
> *are being transformed into the same image from*
> *glory to glory, just as from the Lord,*
> *the Spirit. (2 Corinthians 3:18)*

I love to ask God to let me think of me just as far as I need to for Him to convict me of wrong attitudes or actions, but after that I aim to run back to His feet to marvel at His finished work, fleeing from any interest in self and how well or how poorly I'm doing on this spiritual journey.

Introspection is quicksand. Let's worship God! He alone is worthy of our endless fascination.

For you are great and do marvelous deeds; you alone are God.
PSALM 86:10 NIV

A Hungry Heart Is Needy

My husband slowed the big red machine and stopped, pausing just long enough for me to climb up and take my seat in the cab before he put the header in gear and took off again. I'd called ahead to let him know I was coming to ride the combine with him. Being first a farmer's daughter and then a farmer's wife, I'm well aware that time is always a precious commodity on the farm, but it's at a premium during harvest season when our men are operating under equal parts anxiousness and anticipation. It's a grab bag of emotions that only those who've seen a crop through from infancy to maturity can truly understand. When it's ready, the men work long hours "getting it while the getting's good." It can be hard enough on spouses, but it's even harder on little boys and girls who idolize their daddies.

Years ago my young son was traumatized by just such a harvest season. He was a daddy's boy toddler, dealing poorly with his best big buddy being gone when he woke up and still missing when he went to bed. I can remember Phillip toting around his daddy's work shirt and moaning into the covers of his bunk bed like it was the end of the world as he knew it. And for the record, this didn't make for a picnic for me. When I wasn't taking my son back and forth to the farm for a visit, I was spending large parts of the day trying to convince Phillip that we would all survive the harvest season.

Sometimes we believers remind me of that whining little boy, moping through our days in this life, trying desperately to believe in the promise of the next one when we have the gift of Immanuel, God with us! Yes, Jesus went to heaven, but only after He had prepared a way for us to live in Him now, with the Father, through the Spirit, by His life, death, and resurrection. Jesus said in John 17:25–26:

> *"O righteous Father, although the world has*
> *not known You, yet I have known You; and*
> *these have known that You sent Me; and I have*
> *made Your name known to them, and will*
> *make it known, so that the love with which You*
> *loved Me may be in them, and I in them."*

Jesus promised abundant life this side of heaven to anyone willing to abide in Him—to hold on to His stuff so to speak, to believe, pray, love, and obey. This is one time when clinging isn't just okay; it's recommended.

> *"You are to cling to the LORD your God,*
> *as you have done to this day."*
> JOSHUA 23:8

The closer we get to the cross, the more
room we create there for others.

SATURDAY

A Hungry Heart Is Sharing

I don't care what they say: a person can go home again, if only in her heart. One of my favorite ways of "going home" is to visit my parents' church. Returning to the church I grew up in (second pew, left front) is a lot like sharing a group hug. There is something so very comforting about being among people who knew you through the missing baby teeth, the horn-rimmed glasses of your elementary years, and your supercool high school career. Can I have a witness?

I'm not saying that there haven't been changes at Melbourne Baptist Church over the years. Their recent remodel looks great, and new faces are scattered among the more familiar ones, but for the most part, Melbourne visits always seem like one big déjà vu. My immediate family and I were there not long ago for their Harvest Day. After the song service ended and Mama finished tickling the last ivory key on the piano, she got up gracefully and made her way toward the rest of us. In my mind's eye, I revisited the past and wondered how many times my sisters and I had slid down the same pew to make room for Mama. This time Papa, my married son, my daughter-in-law, my husband, and myself, along with our three grandchildren were the ones doing the adjusting. Let's just say we were sucked up and tucked in. You've done the same thing, haven't you? I imagine you've pulled yourself in to make room for someone before. I'd like to take that memory and show you a beautiful analogy.

Speaking of Jesus, John the Baptist said, "He must increase, but I must decrease" (John 3:30). Basically, John was talking about the ministry of Christ and how important it was for him to prepare the way by getting out of it! I've begun to understand that Jesus is calling us to do the same thing. The way I see it, the more Shellie I can give up, the more room in my family I can offer Jesus to operate. In other words, by a continual effort to submit my little I to the great I Am, I can decrease, so to speak, and in doing so make room for Him in my circle of acquaintances. I'm delightfully challenged by the notion. Do you long to see your family find Christ? If so, I encourage you to draw ever closer to the cross yourself. It's the best way I know to make room for Him in the lives of those you love.

And I pray that the fellowship of your faith may become effective through the knowledge of every good thing which is in you for Christ's sake.

PHILEMON 1:6

Society will never be able to restrict
the words of God written on our
hearts and in our actions.

MONDAY

A Hungry Heart Is Surrendered

Oh, how I love words. This would not be a news flash to my long-time readers and radio listeners, but should validation become necessary, my darling husband would tell one and all that ample proof abounds in the home we share here on the banks of a lake in a town called by God's name.

Here in Lake Providence, words grace our walls, adorn our bookshelves, and call from our throw pillows. There are funny signs, like the gift from my best friend hanging in the laundry room and proudly proclaiming, A SKINNY GIRL LIVES INSIDE OF ME, BUT I CAN USUALLY SHUT HER UP WITH COOKIES. And there are signs that remind any comers of the house rules: NO WHINING. (While I'm the one who hung that one, I confess to being nailed by it on more than one occasion!) There are over-the-door markers that speak blessings on all who enter and several sayings I've stenciled on our walls, like the one that encourages the reader to trust God's heart when you can't trace His hand. Phil's been known to say that you can read your way from one end of this place to the other. The man speaks truth.

Speaking of truth, in the abundance of words surrounding us, truth is what you read the most as you walk through our home:

solid-gold truth from God's own Word and stirring quotes from people of faith. These are the signs this word lover finds it hardest to resist when I'm out and about. These are the ones my dear man graciously overlooks when I succumb to the temptation to tote 'em home.

I was thinking about all of my signs earlier when I heard someone reporting on yet another instance of God's words being banned from a public place. That grieves me.

If I had my way, the public square would be adorned with God's Word just like our home. And yet I reminded myself, and now I'm reminding you, that the Bible calls believers "living epistles." Here's a truth worthy of sober reflection: if those of us who are called by His name would live His Word and carry it about with us, where society allows God's words to be mounted would be a moot point indeed.

You are our letter, written in our hearts,
known and read by all men.
2 Corinthians 3:2

A Hungry Heart Is Intentional

The infamous heat of our Louisiana summers arrives like a freight train. At this point in my life, my idea of beating the heat is tied to the air conditioner, with very few exceptions—for the beach, my friend's pool, the Sea-Doo, or a float boat ride. It's hard to believe that years ago my sisters and I chose to endure these stifling conditions to play outdoors, but we did. Granted, a little backstory may help explain our "choice." Mama liked to tell us that we could find something to do outside or she would find something fun for us to do inside. As I've said in the past, we were country kids, but we weren't stupid. Mama's concept of a big time usually meant cleaning the bathrooms or straightening our closets.

I'm not saying we weren't ever allowed to come inside. As long as we had a good reason, we were welcome indoors. While Mama never actually spelled out what that might be, we understood it to be a medical emergency involving blood or broken bones. Being thirsty was not considered life threatening, as there was always the water hose.

Experience taught us to let the hose run a minute before partaking. If you've ever tried to drink from a water hose that's been lying in the sun on a hot summer day, you know that the initial stream won't quench your thirst. It will scorch your mouth. Had we not learned to linger, we girls never would have tasted the water that flowed once that hose cooled off, and that would have been a crying shame, since that hose could also offer clean, pure refreshment!

Two different experiences and one source of blessing, such is life. There are people who will tell you that they don't like to read the Bible. They'll say this with mournful finality, too, as if there's no hope of that ever changing. I have a Greek word for such an attitude—*hogwash*! (You're right, that's more like southern Greek, but still.) That excuse reminds me of those water hose moments from my childhood. God Himself tells us in Jeremiah that His Word is like a fire and a hammer, and so it is, but He also describes it as fresh bread, and yes, living water.

I beg you to linger long in the Good Book and give yourself time in the scriptures until your desire for God's Word deepens and the Word begins to quench your strongest thirst. Given time, our parched hearts come to find that God's Word is the only source that truly satisfies.

"The afflicted and needy are seeking water, but there is none, and their tongue is parched with thirst; I, the LORD, will answer them Myself, as the God of Israel I will not forsake them."

ISAIAH 41:17

A Hungry Heart Is Praying

I have a friend named Tanya (short *a*) from southern Louisiana and a friend named Tanya (short *o*) from north Louisiana who spell their names the same exact way but pronounce them differently.

Please don't tell them this, because it's embarrassing, but their name game causes me great confusion. I know what you're thinking, and you're right. A belle should know how to pronounce her friends' names, especially when she's known Tanya (short *a*) for umpteen dozen years and Tanya (short *o*) for more than a decade. And yet when the phone rings, and it's one of them, I find it necessary to stop and think before I can greet her! The last thing I want is to offend either of them!

The confusion intensified when I found myself praying a lot for Short *A* Tanya when she lost her job, home, and car to historic flooding at the same time I was praying for Short *O* Tanya because she has experienced more loss in her life than I can wrap my head around and is still seeking God. Every time I brought their names to Father God, I'd have to stop and think, lest I confused myself.

My saving tip was a certain little epiphany that *a* comes before *o*, and I've known Short *A* Tanya longer than Short *O*

Tanya. It helped. A little.

Sad, isn't it? If you haven't quit reading even though you're convinced I'm not playing with a full deck—and who's to say you don't have a case?—I'd like to say thank you and close out this rather embarrassing devotional with a reassuring truth. The God who hears my prayers isn't the least confused by the pronunciation of my friends' names. John 10:3 says, "He calls his own sheep by name and leads them out."

Thankfully, you and I can bring our prayer requests to God's throne and wait before Him in confident assurance that He hears us, even in our less-than-clearheaded moments. For the One who is intimately acquainted with all our joys and all our sorrows calls us by name and loves us one and all.

It is good to hope and wait patiently
for the LORD's salvation.
LAMENTATIONS 3:26 ISV

THURSDAY

A Hungry Heart Is Celebrating

Pranking your BFF can be great fun, but there are things you should know.

You could come home from a road trip to find plastic bugs hidden around your house because your revenge-minded BFF has gained entry to your home. You may live on edge in your own home wondering where the next plastic roach and/or spider could be lurking. And you may think your dearly beloved Dixie Belle had a doggy accident in your bedroom while you were away, when it's really a mound of disgusting plastic.

Yes, all of these things have recently befallen me, and more.

Shortly after I began discovering these prizes, I ran into my BFF's mother, and she apologized for her daughter's behavior before asking innocently, "So, did you ever find the bat?"

Bat? We were interrupted by another friend, but I left our unfinished conversation thinking surely she was joking. Surely there wasn't a bat in my house. Wrong, Shirley. After spending a week on full alert for the little guy, wondering if he was dead, alive, or plastic, I sort of relaxed. Silly me. Days later I reached my bedroom early enough to read instead of falling in bed comatose like that old-fashioned Nestea plunge, only to be startled by a nasty fake bat hiding under my lamp shade. I had little problem staying awake to read that night.

Have I found everything she planted? Who knows? Just yesterday I discovered Pedro the Panty Python in my lingerie drawer, complete with an introductory name tag tied around his neck. This prank seems to be the gift that keeps on giving, and not in a good way. On the other hand, that very line moves me to a great celebration.

Would you join me in praising the unparalleled present that God offered the whole world on an old rugged cross? Far from being hidden or obscured, God's only begotten Son was lifted high on a cross for all to see, the story of His empty tomb was spread far and wide, and the life He purchased for us has no end. Jesus rescues us, and then He rewards us for simply embracing that redemption. In every single way, He really is the gift that keeps on giving.

Thanks be to God for His indescribable gift!
2 CORINTHIANS 9:15

FRIDAY

A Hungry Heart Is Needy

My parents are big on the importance of keeping a vehicle's gas tank as close to full as possible. They will top off a tank in a New York minute. This could be because they've always lived in the country where there isn't a gas station on every corner, or on any corner, for that matter. And it may just be a generational thing, but to my parents' way of thinking, when the needle gets anywhere around the halfway mark, a person is running on empty.

Papa and Mama have plenty of reasons for keeping their gas tank full, but the number one reason to stay topped off is so that they will be prepared in case of an emergency. They have done their dead-level best to transfer this type of foresight to me. "What if you have to go to the hospital in the middle of the night, hmm? Ever thought about that, Shellie Charlene?"

I, of course, rarely if ever think about things like that. I'm not at all proud of that trait, mind you. My goal is to grow up to be a plan-ahead type of person, but so far it just isn't happening.

Fortunately, my beloved hubby is on the same page with the folks. He's good about reminding me to top off my tank, too, largely because he knows how easy it would be for me to travel without giving fuel, or the lack of it, a second thought until it's too late. Again, I'm not saying that's a good thing. Everyone knows you can't get where you're going without fuel in the tank, right? Well, yes and no.

Oh, sure, we recognize the importance of fuel where our vehicles are concerned, but when it comes to our spirits, we are slower to see the danger of driving on empty. How tragic that we would willingly coast on the fumes of a Sunday sermon when we need Jesus so today, and we each have been given the privilege of keeping our tanks topped off by nourishing ourselves in His Word and in His presence. Come on, y'all. Let's live full to overflowing.

"This book of the law shall not depart from your mouth, but you shall meditate on it day and night, so that you may be careful to do according to all that is written in it; for then you will make your way prosperous, and then you will have success."

JOSHUA 1:8

SATURDAY

A Hungry Heart Is Sharing

My southern mama couldn't have been more than forty years old when she began discussing who should have what when she was gone. It's not something my sisters and I wanted to talk about, but she couldn't be dissuaded! Mama insisted that she wasn't trying to be morbid, and I believe her. Southerners are just big on heritage. Discussing what one will pass down when one passes on comes as natural to us as breathing. Even if they don't have treasured antiques from past generations, almost everyone has sentimental possessions to bequeath, as well as a valuable store of hand-me-down wisdom they hope to send down the line.

The wisdom I'm talking about is not just the southern sayings we've all come to love, such as, "If you find yourself in a hole, the first thing to do is stop digging," or "Don't corner something meaner than you." I'm referring rather to those acquired skills we get from our elders, such as the art of stretching groceries so no one's the wiser, and how to set a hook in the mouth of a hungry fish. Our elders have a lot of important lessons to teach us if we'll listen. My husband, Phil, has learned a lot about farming from his father. My son has now graduated from college, settled down, started a family, and joined the farming operation full-time.

Fortunately for him, he benefits from the store of knowledge Phil has gotten from his dad, along with the wisdom Phil has acquired from his own experiences, and he is that much further ahead.

Surely that's the goal of good parents everywhere, to give their children everything they can for a better life. It's a worthy goal, too, unless our efforts are spent entirely on temporary things to the exclusion of eternal truths that won't rust, grow old, or fade away. We all want what's best for our children, but if, in all of our teaching, we don't lead them toward faith in God through Jesus His Son, our other lessons, however thorough, will be taught in vain.

Deuteronomy 29:29 says, "The secret things belong to the LORD our God, but the things revealed belong to us and to our children forever" (NIV). Awesome! The truths we uncover about God in His Word, the ones that come alive to us, belong to our children and grandchildren, too! That's enough reason to apply ourselves right there! Come on, folks. Have you found Him? He's in the Book. Our kids need a heritage of faith, and we can't share what we don't have.

All Scripture is inspired by God and profitable for teaching, for reproof, for correction, for training in righteousness; so that the man of God may be adequate, equipped for every good work.
2 TIMOTHY 3:16–17

A Hungry Heart Is Surrendered

My son was a teenager when he permanently injured a finger on my right hand. Oh, not intentionally. Phillip was just a growing man-child, feeling his oats about the weight and inches he'd put on that summer, and one of his favorite new activities was engaging his mother in a game of Uncle.

You've probably played Uncle a time or two yourself, but for the sake of making sure we're all on the same page, Phillip and I were finger wrestling that day. That's where you intertwine your fingers with your opponents and each of you tries to bend the other person's digits back until someone can't take it anymore and cries out for relief. I freely admit to crying "uncle" that day, and yet I was still left with a memento from the occasion. That finger on my right hand I mentioned earlier—it hasn't been the same since.

Can I tell you that my idea of surrendering to Jesus used to be something like that game of Uncle with Phillip? I saw surrendering as someone struggling and struggling and eventually relinquishing the fight to a stronger foe. And, of course, Jesus is a stronger foe, and I was right to want to surrender to Him; but I could never figure out how to take the act of surrendering beyond theory and into practice.

I understood that I must decrease to see Him increase in my life. I just needed someone to tell me how to do that, exactly. I needed verbs! Surrendering felt like an abstract, elusive idea I couldn't put my finger on other than to say, "I give" over and over again, and that was a well-intentioned cycle of defeat that led nowhere. Is anybody tracking with me?

Over time, and after repeatedly bringing this issue to God in prayer, I've begun to get a different image of surrendering, and it's transforming my life. I now see that the more I invite Him into the everyday, common moments of my life, the easier I find it to surrender my will to His. Why? Because I've found that the more time I spend with Him, the less time I can spend without Him; and now I want to do His will because I value being near Him.

Fascinating, isn't it? The little *i* in each of us that wants to dictate our way loses the ability to dominate our life when Christ is our focus. How precious is the finished work of Christ. He really did do it all, and we can learn to surrender by simply beholding.

For I am confident of this very thing, that He who began a good work in you will perfect it until the day of Christ Jesus.

PHILIPPIANS 1:6

TUESDAY

A Hungry Heart Is Intentional

When it comes to trimming our shrubs and trees, my darling man and I have vastly different ideas on when to say *when*. Phil loves to prune. He takes it to a legendary extreme. I can almost hear the foliage begin to whimper whenever the man picks up yard clippers. I would say that Phil is a "more is more" type of pruner.

On the other hand, Phil would tell you that I am anti-pruning. He would say that if it were possible, I'd be perfectly willing to let the landscape around us grow up and over the house. The truth would lie somewhere in between.

It's not the War of the Roses or anything, but the man and I have learned a lot about handling these seasonal skirmishes. Over the years, we've worked out our roles. Phil trims while I pick up the discarded limbs and supervise—I mean *observe*. This method allows us to negotiate during the process instead of sparring afterward.

I don't mind admitting that I find spiritual pruning even less enjoyable than seeing my chrysanthemums receiving an overzealous makeover, but I am convinced that it's infinitely more necessary.

Jesus tells us in John 15 that He is the Vine and we are the branches, and that His Father prunes every branch that bears fruit so it might bring forth more fruit!

More fruit? Now we're talking. Isn't that what we all want? It gets better. Jesus goes on to say that we're cleaned through His Word. Did you know that word *cleaned* has the same Greek meaning as the word *pruned*? In other words, if we'll learn from God's Word and yield to Him, Father can use His scriptures to prune us instead of having to let us face harsher circumstances. It is in resisting Him that we find ourselves learning tough lessons the hard way.

Here's a closing thought that makes me smile. The Father, Son, and Holy Spirit are in total agreement over our development, yours and mine, and what needs to be trimmed and when. No cutting now and regretting it later. Now that deserves an amen!

The grace of the Lord Jesus Christ, and the love of God,
and the fellowship of the Holy Spirit, be with you all.
2 CORINTHIANS 13:14

God often asks us to step
down from our solution so
we can kneel down in His.

WEDNESDAY

A Hungry Heart Is Praying

It wasn't the first time I tried to use my superpowers, but as far as I can remember, it may have been the first time I actually wore an honest-to-goodness cape. I had good reason. My friend was in a state of serious emotional distress. This was no time for indecision, people! I had no sooner hung up the phone than I knew exactly what it was I had to do.

I promptly took a large beach towel, marked it with a big bold *S*, tied it around my shoulders, and dashed to her rescue. My superpowers didn't change a single thing that day, no not one, but the cape did give my friend some good laughs. No harm, no foul, at least not that time. Sadly, this hasn't always been the case. I'm afraid I could list a lot more instances where my determination to be superwoman in a loved one's life has only exacerbated the problem.

You may not wear a cape, but I would dare to say that you've ridden to a few rescues of your own. None of us like to see those we love stuck between a rock and a hard place, nor do we enjoy the helpless feeling we are stuck with when we find that we are powerless to change their circumstances.

Of course, from a purely theological standpoint, most believers would probably agree that God often uses difficult situations to bring people to the saving knowledge of Jesus Christ. The concept is just easier to swallow when the difficult situations don't involve people we know and love. When it's our people, our neat little theories get sorely tested because it requires us Supermamas, Superdads, Superfriends, and Supersiblings to trust God with the eternal picture instead of trying to help Him out with the present one.

No one likes to see people they love in pain, whether physical or emotional, but as believers, we are challenged to believe that God can, and is, using those difficulties for His purposes. So how do we know when it's the right time to get involved and when we should give our superhero horses a much-needed rest? I can't answer that question, and I'm not even tempted to try. What I can tell you is that there is one course of action that's right in every situation. God never asks us to get out of the way in order to sit down, but rather to kneel down and join Him in the solution.

Let us therefore come boldly unto the throne of grace, that we may obtain mercy, and find grace to help in time of need.
Hebrews 4:16 kjv

THURSDAY

A Hungry Heart Is Celebrating

In my very first book, *Lessons Learned on Bull Run Road*, I wrote about my summer love affair with the bookmobile from the East Carroll Parish Library. For a little book lover at the end of a long dirt road, miles from a public library, that busload of books lumbering down our country road looked like a traveling amusement park. Granted, I did have a problem with the bookmobile's rule of six books per child, but I soon found a way around that, too. I'd do chores for my sisters in exchange for their book count, since they weren't all fired up about reading, anyway. Score!

Picture mini-me headed back up the drive with my mother lode—eighteen books. Life was good.

Now fast-forward with me, if you will. It appears my little radio talk show, *ATS LIVE*, has garnered the attention of book publicists everywhere, as they are sending me books by the boatload. Please hear me: I don't think this is because I'm setting the world on fire with my Monday evening talk show as much as it is about the extreme volume of books on the market out there and the driving need for today's authors to get their work in front of the eyes and ears of potential readers.

Still, whatever the reason, practically every single workday a big brown truck lumbers down my long driveway and a sweet fellow gets out and hands me books. Free books. Do you see the pattern? I didn't. Not for the longest time, anyway.

And then one day I was walking back inside with a stack of freshly delivered books when literally out of the blue two words fell into my heart: "You're welcome." Just that quickly, the scene around me faded and I was rooted to the spot. Tears flooded my eyes as I thought about that mini-me longing for books and this grown-up me awash in 'em.

I share this story, dear reader, to celebrate the incredible intimacy of our heavenly Father who sees the end from the beginning. I'm His favorite. And so are you. And you, and you, and you.

He knows us, one and all. He knows what makes us tick and what ticks us off—and He loves us, everyone. Oh, how He loves us. Oh.

"For God so loved the world that He gave
His only begotten Son, that whoever believes in
Him should not perish but have everlasting life."
JOHN 3:16 NKJV

FRIDAY

A Hungry Heart Is Needy

"Here, Keggie," my granddaughter said. "Hold my frog, please. I don't want to lose it." It would be a waste of time for anyone to tell Emerson she shouldn't play with frogs. That ship has sailed. And for the record, this Keggie complied.

You may or may not share Emerson's fondness of frogs, but I'm guessing we all know what it means to trust someone to hold our treasures, right? So it occurred to me that this might be a good way to explain a spiritual principle that I've had trouble articulating.

Let me be completely honest. I need Jesus in the worst way every day. I can't even commit to taking a certain attitude about a particular issue and then keep that attitude without resorting to Him for reinforcement. I used to feel bad about asking Him to help me love someone I found unlovable if I had already asked Him for that particular grace a dozen times before. Not anymore. I've finally learned to embrace the fact that there's nothing good in me apart from Christ, because my deficiencies cause me to stay near my Source!

Ephesians 1:3 reads, "Blessed be the God and Father of our Lord Jesus Christ, who has blessed us with every spiritual blessing in the heavenly places in Christ." While those unlimited blessings are indeed ours, do note that we don't have them in ourselves. Jesus is holding them for us!

If you've ever wondered what it means to have your gaze fixed on Jesus as you go about your daily life, this is it. Jesus is holding all the precious spiritual blessings you need for whatever arises. That means all the patience, hope, peace, love, and strength you need to meet the demands of the day are in Him, and that's just to name a few spiritual blessings of an infinite list. Victory is learning to reach for what we need when we need it.

For of His fullness we have all received,
and grace upon grace.

JOHN 1:16

SATURDAY

A Hungry Heart Is Sharing

One evening, my friend River Jordan and I sat down to enjoy a much-anticipated meal together at a particular restaurant in a town I won't mention by name. It was the close of a very long day on the road during a book tour that had us taking in something like seventy-nine cities in fifty-eight days. Okay, that might be a slight exaggeration, but we really were making some tracks. I mention the schedule to set the mood. River and I were at the point of exhaustion where everything was funnier than it should have been. Got it? Okay, cue the next scene.

As we were finishing our meal, the cute young waiter returned and asked if he could tell us about the evening's desserts. "Sure," we said, probably in unison.

The waiter took a deep breath and began. "Tonight," he said, "we have brownies."

River and I waited. Our waiter waited, too. We waited some more. As did he. It finally began to dawn on us that he was through. There was no further description forthcoming to make us want what they had to offer. No ode to a delicate pastry and a melt-in-your-mouth frosting. No mention of toasted pecans adorning the top. They had brownies. Show over.

River and I were unable to contain ourselves, but let it be known that we did apologize for laughing out loud, and we did leave the young fellow a hearty tip for entertainment if nothing else.

I often think that we, as believers, fall just as short with our description of why someone should seek the God we serve as our young waiter did with those brownies. We talk vaguely of eternity and some future reward. While those things are true and worthy of celebration, such a lame sketch falls woefully short of what it means to live this life with the Spirit of the living Lord as our Counselor, Friend, and Comforter and with the everlasting God leading us home! Have mercy. We could never exhaust this subject, but with the Holy Spirit's help, we can live trying. Can I get an amen?

"But you will receive power when the Holy Spirit has come upon you; and you shall be My witnesses both in Jerusalem, and in all Judea and Samaria, and even to the remotest part of the earth."

ACTS 1:8

MONDAY

A Hungry Heart Is Surrendered

Timing is a perpetual concern on the farm, and it's never at more of a premium than it is when you're trying to get your crop in the ground (unless it's time to get it out!). The men are always looking to find the optimum planting time so they can strike while the iron is hot. Experience has taught them that strike two, if necessary, will be that much more tenuous. Take corn, for instance. Planting too late means risking the ears tasseling out in the heat of the summer and stunting the yield.

I remember one particular year when less-than-ideal weather conditions produced a spotty stand of corn and consequently set up a most unpleasant scenario on our farm. I remember my heart going out to my husband the morning he described to me what they were about to do that day. I sipped my coffee and listened to him describe how they would use a spray rig to kill the spotty young corn that was standing while simultaneously planting the new seed, the idea being that doing both in one pass would save precious time and fuel. The expression on Phil's face hurt me. This farmer's wife knew it went against my man's grain, no pun intended, to destroy his own crop, but I also knew that he was doing the right thing. Leaving the older plants in the field would just make competition for the new crop and end up stunting its growth, too.

It hurts to give up something that has your name on it. I know, because I've often tried to add God's ways onto my own. I can assure you that such a plan only leads to a bad case of stunted growth. An abundant life in Christ is available to all, but it's nonnegotiable—you must give up yours to have His. Consider these words from the late theologian E. M. Bounds: "God takes nothing by halves. He gives nothing by halves. We can have the whole of Him when He has the whole of us."

Pulling up our lives to make room for Christ's can be painful, but it comes with a payoff that is too priceless to measure. The more of me I give up, the more aware I am of His abiding presence. That's not just a sweet trade, friends. It's the deal of a lifetime.

"Whoever wishes to save his life will lose it;
but whoever loses his life for My sake will find it."
MATTHEW 16:25

TUESDAY

A Hungry Heart Is Intentional

I heard a joke once about a little girl who was hurrying down a sidewalk on her way to Sunday school. I'm fuzzy on the details, but when has that stopped me from telling a story? (That was rhetorical, y'all.) Seriously, I'm pretty sure I can set this up for us, and I know it's worth a try. I see a message embedded in the humor and that happens to be my favorite kind of tale to tell!

The way I heard it, the little girl was trying to avoid being late for class again, which would be the second Sunday in a row. It didn't look good, however, which is why she decided to pray while she ran.

"Lord," she began, "help me get to church on time. Please!"

Just then, the little girl tripped and fell on the hard pavement. Now she was late, her knees were skinned up, and her tights were torn. Frustrated, the girl could be heard saying, "Thanks, Lord, but You didn't have to push!"

There's the humor. Now here's the message. The truth is that our Father leads those who believe; and He guides those who respond, but He doesn't push. Consider the words of Jesus from John 10:27: "My sheep hear My voice, and I know them, and they follow Me."

Sometimes we believers tend to think we don't hear Him near as well as He said we would, but the problem is always on our end, friends. God is willing to speak to us through His Word, but we must choose to open it! God has also made it possible for us to hear Him by coming to live in us through the Holy Spirit. Learning to be led by the Spirit of God is about yielding when we believe He is speaking, and yielding quickly. The quicker we determine to obey Him, the more developed our hearing skills become and the easier it is to hear Him speak the next time.

Trust and obey—that ought to be a song. Oh, you're right. Cue the choir and let's do this thing!

"Now therefore, O sons, listen to me,
for blessed are they who keep my ways."
PROVERBS 8:32

WEDNESDAY

A Hungry Heart Is Praying

I hope this disclosure won't negatively affect my official title as Belle of All Things Southern, but in more than twenty years of married life, I can count on two hands the number of times I've actually fried chicken for my family. Sorry, it's just too easy to let fast food satisfy that craving without the kitchen mess, which makes me want to give Mama due props for all the fried chicken of my childhood. We ate a lot of chicken on Bull Run Road, and it didn't come from a takeout box downtown, but the coop out back.

Most people would think raising three daughters wouldn't require as big a grocery bill as bringing up a house full of boys. Mama would say, "Not so fast." Like anything else, that would be determined by the appetite of the girls in question, and my sisters and I brought some hearty ones to the table. When fried chicken was on the menu, two birds gave up their ghosts to make it happen.

Once our appetites were somewhat sated, we'd engage in some supper table fun called "Who's got the pulley bone?" Also called the wishbone, the pulley bone game was played by two kids holding on to each end, each making a silent wish, and then breaking the bone. The one with the longest bone was supposed to have her wish come true. I wouldn't know. My oldest sister,

Cyndie, always won. I never knew how she rigged that, but if you knew Cyndie, you'd know she rigged it.

I thought about the pulley bone earlier. In Luke 18:1 Jesus prefaces the story of the persistent widow with this straight-up announcement: "I'm about to tell you a story so you'll always pray and not lose heart." And just like that, Jesus makes it abundantly clear that He'd like to see us big people get a backbone—a prayer backbone, and leave the wishing for the little ones!

> *Yet those who wait for the LORD will gain new strength;*
> *they will mount up with wings like eagles, they will run*
> *and not get tired, they will walk and not become weary.*
>
> ISAIAH 40:31

THURSDAY

A Hungry Heart Is Celebrating

My man understands me. He realizes I don't choose to be forgetful; but with me, it is what it is. How about a story for illustration? Whenever we get at that milestone moment in our marriage that requires us to begin shopping for a new vehicle, I try my best to bow out of the picture. Quite honestly, I don't like the process. Needing a new vehicle would be Phil's phrasing anyway; I think it's too strong. If it were left up to me I wouldn't think I needed a new vehicle until the wheels fell off the old one. And yet my husband, blessed pragmatist, will begin looking at the miles on whatever road-weary car I'm driving at the time and begin worrying that something much like that may indeed happen when I'm on the road alone. And that, dear ones, was just background to set up the story.

A couple years ago now, I found myself returning a car I'd been test-driving to the good folks at Jim Taylor Chevrolet. It was late evening. I arrived at the dealership, an hour's drive from my house, well after closing time. Fortunately, they'd already told me where to leave the new car's keys if that happened.

I pulled in and parked beside my trusty Tahoe. She looked so familiar I had a moment of nostalgia, followed closely by panic when I reached into my purse for my old keys. No ma'am. I couldn't have left them at home! More searching—apparently I could and I did. I debated calling Phil or taking the new car back home. On one hand, I'd promised to return it Monday evening. I didn't feel right putting more miles on it. On the other hand, I wondered how weary my knight in shining armor was growing of rescuing his dim-witted damsel. In the end, I did call, and my knight rode up, yet again, with the keys and without any fussing or attitude, just wearing that patient smile that says, *I know you can't help it.*

Driving home, I considered my forgetfulness and used it to celebrate the wonder of our omniscient God who forgets on purpose! God's Word tells us that if our sins have been forgiven in Christ Jesus, He no longer remembers them. That's not just forgetting; that's a deliberate act of an all-knowing God not to recall the offense. If someone has been reminding you of your past, don't assume it's God. If you're forgiven, it's forgotten!

For I will be merciful to their wrongdoing,
and I will never again remember their sins.
HEBREWS 8:12 HCSB

We must relinquish the sheer force of
our wills to benefit from the priceless
truth of God's Word.

A Hungry Heart Is Needy

I've often used the camera on my phone to take pictures of my grandson drawing one of his beloved trucks. I like to videotape Grant's work, too. That may sound like overkill, but I want to have evidence of our pint-sized Picasso at work that documents his age along with the artwork. Seriously, he's that good.

Grant prefers paper now, but when he was younger he created on one of those drawing toys that look like an Etch A Sketch, only it comes with an attached pencil rather than little wheels. May I add here that I feel this is a huge improvement over that red toy of my childhood? Sorry, Etch A Sketch. I never did appreciate having to draw in one continuous line. I found it extremely limiting. And yet that's very often how Grant creates. He'll draw a truck with incredible detail without once lifting his pencil. I don't know a thing about art. And yet because I am southern and thus fond of signs, I'm certain this is a sign of something.

Grant is quite a perfectionist about his art. He'll start over in a heartbeat if his drawing isn't progressing to suit him. Back in the days when he used his drawing toy, he employed a curious style to delete his work. Instead of bothering with the affixed slider that's supposed to erase the board, Grant developed the habit of beating on the drawing board with his little hand when he wanted an image to go away.

When I think of how Grant slammed on his drawing to erase his efforts I'm reminded of us big people, you and me big, God-believing type of people. Many times we'll try to banish our ugly thoughts, bad memories, and nagging worries through the sheer force of our own wills. That works about as well as trying not to think about a pink elephant. (Admit it. Your mind just produced a pastel pachyderm.)

While we're at it, we would all benefit from a similar confession. We can't hammer our thoughts into submission the way Grant once banged on his drawings to delete them either. And yet, praise God, there is a way to drain our thoughts of their power even as we renew our strength. Praise the name of Jesus—if we confess our need of Him, He is more than willing to help us learn to reroute our thoughts by countering them with the priceless truth of God's Word. Somebody needs to say, "Amen!"

The peace of God, which surpasses all comprehension,
will guard your hearts and your minds in Christ Jesus.
PHILIPPIANS 4:7

A Hungry Heart Is Sharing

Here in the South we have a good old saying that describes a super stubborn person. We say that type of person will "argue with a signpost." When my sisters and I were growing up, we heard Papa use this line more than a few times about one cousin of ours in particular. I'm going to change his name to protect the not-so-innocent. We'll go with Cousin Willie.

When it came to a good debate, Cousin Willie didn't know when to say when. It was almost like a hobby with him. Let someone comment that the sun was out and Cousin Willie would take a scientific position and argue that actually, the sun never goes "in," so it couldn't really be out. It would've been one level of irritating if Cousin Willie had chosen a stance and left it there, but he couldn't let a subject rest without having the last word; hence his reputation for arguing with a signpost.

I often think about that cousin when I see Facebook debates over spiritual matters. I'm not going to get specific here because I don't want to encourage other signpost-prone people who may be reading. Instead, I want to leave you with something to think about. It's impossible to seek the friendship of Jesus in an ongoing and determined way and not be transformed over time in the process. If we're following Jesus, we should be in the process of changing from the inside out, or as 2 Corinthians 3:18–20 reads, "We all, with unveiled face, beholding as in a mirror the glory of the Lord, are being transformed into the same image from glory to glory, just as from the Lord, the Spirit."

But we won't convince anyone that Christ lives in us through heated debate. Debating spiritual matters with skeptics is like a bird trying to prove to an earthbound animal that it can fly while they're both sitting on the ground. The most compelling proof is for the bird simply to take off and fly.

For those whom He foreknew, He also predestined to become conformed to the image of His Son, so that He would be the firstborn among many brethren.
ROMANS 8:29

A Hungry Heart Is Surrendered

It happened years ago, but I remember that day vividly. My sisters and I could barely contain ourselves as we waited for Papa to finish checking us in at the front desk. We were on vacation with our parents during a season of our lives when hotel swimming pools were considered more like the prime destination than a temporary diversion. At that moment, we were standing on one side of a beautiful wrought iron gate staring at the Olympic-size pool visible on the other side, and the beautiful blue water was calling our names! So was Mama, who was growing increasingly hesitant about our accommodations.

"Girls, get back over here!" she called. And then she turned her attention to Papa who had just returned to the car with a room key and a big grin. "Ed," she said, "we can't go in there looking like this."

We girls looked at each other. This was odd. We looked just like we always looked on vacation: shorts, tanks, and flip-flops.

"Just look at that!" Mama exclaimed, as a long, sleek limousine pulled up and a couple of the high-priced hotel's paying customers stepped out in style. Whoa, Nellie!

We weren't paying guests, but we weren't freeloading either. Earlier that afternoon we had tried to check in at a much more reasonable establishment that was holding our reservations. Unfortunately for them, they had suffered a severe plumbing problem and were having to locate backup lodging for all their guests. Fortunately for us, there was a convention in town, and the only rooms left were at this place, which to our young eyes, looked like the Taj Mahal. To honor their commitment, and because all other lodging was booked, the more economical hotel was now having to set us up in style—at their cost.

"Oh, we're going in," Papa said. "It's paid for." And so we did. I daresay Mama ended up enjoying the hotel room's luxurious amenities every bit as much as we girls enjoyed that pool.

Granted, it seems strange for anyone not to be eager to go first class at another person's expense, but it happens, and I'm not just talking hotels and swimming pools now. Countless believers are headed to heaven and willing to settle here on earth for the worn-out comfort of yesteryear's conversion experience, when Jesus is offering the upgrade of an abundant life.

The offer is ironclad, only we can't have our wills and His way. An intimate relationship with Jesus lies on the other side of complete surrender. The promise of abundant life is within our reach, but we'll have to lay self aside to find it.

"But seek first His kingdom and His righteousness,
and all these things will be added to you."
MATTHEW 6:33

*If we'll fix our gaze and
watch the path of our feet,
our ways will be established.*

TUESDAY

A Hungry Heart Is Intentional

My sisters and I grew up on a farm in rural Louisiana. We were blessed with free time to amuse ourselves and plenty of wide-open countryside to act out whatever our imaginations could invent. Papa's fuel tanks became our inexhaustible horses. We cowgirls saddled them up to fight and prevail over bands of warring Indians. Cane poles lining our ditches were stripped and used as building materials in the construction of what we considered to be elaborate forts, worthy of overnight stays. (Unfortunately, Mama was the building inspector, and our efforts fell short of her required code for adequate lodging.)

We were also fond of any and all activities requiring a good sense of balance. Ponytailed daredevils, we graduated from climbing trees to exploring the roof of Papa's tractor shed and walking the rails of the bridge by our house. I recently had a déjà vu moment watching a fellow adventurer tightrope walking between those tall buildings in Chicago. Oh, sure, his audience was larger, and the danger he faced was graver, but still I identified with his slow and steady movements, one foot placed carefully in front of the other. Focus is everything for us high-wire performers.

All joking aside, as I watched the high-wire performer

walking very intentionally, with his eyes straight ahead, I thought of Proverbs 4:25–26, where we're instructed to give our attention to God's words and not let them drift from our sight, for from them flows life itself! We're told to let our eyes look directly ahead and our gaze be fixed straight in front of us, to watch the path of our feet so that all of our ways will be established.

Eyes fixed, gazed focused—it sounds serious because it is. The dangers of not living intentionally in God's ways are even graver than the consequences of ambling aimlessly across a high wire far above city streets.

We each are given the choice of whether we will live with our hearts wide open and our ears deliberately attuned to Jesus. We can choose to ignore the noise of our world and listen for the holy, or we can turn a deaf ear to Jesus, the Word of God who took on flesh. But be warned: to be apart from Him is death; to live in Him is life forevermore.

He who has the Son has the life; he who does
not have the Son of God does not have the life.
1 JOHN 5:12

WEDNESDAY

A Hungry Heart Is Praying

"I'm telling!"

The singsong phrase transported me back to elementary school. Here was a threat I hadn't heard in a while. I looked down at my little boy and laughed.

"And just who are you going to tell?" I asked. My son's big blue-green eyes met mine. "Nanee!" he said, seriously. "You're getting all of her stuff." At the time of Phillip's announcement, we were standing in his grandmother's kitchen, where I had just helped myself to a bottle of water and some snack crackers after letting myself in with the extra key. Now I understood why Phillip had passed on the juice box I offered him from the refrigerator. He wasn't interested in being a part of my perceived crime.

I told him I was going to leave Nanee a note to tell her we'd come by while she was out, but Phillip remained skeptical. He was more concerned with the liberties I was taking with his grandmother's belongings than he was with my good intentions; and he wasn't falling for my explanations of how Nanee wouldn't mind and her kitchen would always be mine.

Today that little tattletale, who once accused me of breaking and entering my own mother's house, is a six-foot-two married man with a wife and three children of his own; and believe me here, he is as comfortable ransacking my refrigerator as he is the one at his house. Phillip is secure in the knowledge that this will always be his home and he'll always be welcome to share whatever blessings his dad and I can offer.

Our heavenly Father offers a similar blessing to His kids, and by that I mean that what's His is ours through the gift of His Son. And yet many believers often have as limited and confused an understanding of those benefits as Phillip once had about my right to help myself in Nanee's kitchen. The secret that opens the understanding is fellowship.

See, I was assured of my access to my parents' house because I was confident of and secure in the relationship I had with them, and as Phillip grew up he matured in the same understanding. In a similar way, it is through a maturing relationship with the Father that a believer comes to understand the blessings of his or her salvation. Spend time with Him in His Word and in prayer, and you'll say it this way: "I know whom I have believed, and what is His is mine."

Of His fullness we have all received.

JOHN 1:16

THURSDAY

A Hungry Heart Is Celebrating

My best friend and I were traveling when we pulled off the interstate and into a handy drugstore for a few necessities and a pit stop. We were checking out the deep wrinkle cream (for Red) and brown spot fade cream (for me) when I realized I'd just left my cell phone in the bathroom. I quickly ran back to retrieve it but, alas, it was already gone! Only three, maybe four, minutes had passed and someone had picked it up!

As I reported the missing phone to management, praying someone was turning it in, Red began trailing our prime suspect, having zeroed in on a suspicious-acting female, the only customer we'd seen come out of the restroom after me. Without making wild accusations, we had one of the clerks ask our unidentified suspect if she'd seen a cell phone in the restroom. The unsub denied involvement. Red looked at me and rolled her eyes from our eavesdropping position nearby. In our ensuing investigation, we tried turning up the heat by letting the unsub overhear us talking about the phone's GPS, but we still couldn't crack her. (Yes, there is a chance that we have watched too many detective shows. How could you tell?) In the end, we had no recourse but to make yet another detour by the po-po to report the theft.

As you can imagine, I was bummed about the theft of what is effectively my second brain and the possibility of losing all the information I had stored in it. Honest confession from your humble writer: it took a few miles and a prayer session with my traveling buddy, but as the afternoon wore on, God answered my requests for perspective and resettled my soul.

I'm so thankful for the baby born in Bethlehem who grew into a carpenter and became the Savior of all who will call on Him. He is indeed the Prince of Peace! Today I want to celebrate with you the preciousness of His Carpenter's level. How faithfully He aligns the bubbles of our hearts when we yield our hearts to Him. How faithful He is to even out our most ragged emotions and bring us peace. Come, let us adore Him.

Come, let us worship and bow down,
let us kneel before the LORD our Maker.

PSALM 95:6

FRIDAY

A Hungry Heart Is Needy

My kids had them. My grandkids have them. I'm talking about their "lovies." The textbook definition of a lovie is any object, often a stuffed animal or blanket, that wee ones form an emotional attachment to in order to feel safe and comfort themselves. This practice is known as self-soothing.

Horses, giraffes, doggies, and rabbits—the lovies of my kids and now my grandkids have taken many forms. Back in the day, my toddler son was devoted to a well-worn blanket that sported one bundled-up corner of wadded matting. Phillip considered this to be blankey's head, and he once had a complete meltdown because some totally innocent person accidentally sat on blankey's face. Her name is not important here.

For the most part, a child's bond with a lovie and his or her ability to use it to self-soothe can be a good thing. But do take care. If your child is bonded to a lovie, do not—and I repeat, do not—lose said lovie if you value peace on earth.

Here's another warning. As Christians, we need to be mindful not to develop our own little lovies out of otherwise wonderful spiritual disciplines like church attendance, prayer, and/or our individual Bible studies. Why would I say such a thing? Because

I know from my own experience that it's possible to use these things as security blankets to self-soothe ourselves right out of God's fellowship by using them to feel right with God instead of seeing them as tools to grow closer to Him.

This may sound like a fine line, but give it some thought before you arbitrarily discard the idea. Our spiritual disciplines are good and wholly necessary, but if we aren't seeking God in them, we're creating self-soothing lovies. We need Jesus! No amount of reading, praying, or churchgoing can save our souls; and no amount of such spiritual disciplines can sustain our souls if we're checking them off instead of using them to hear God for ourselves and, in hearing, to respond with obedience. They aren't the real thing. He is.

"I am the way, the truth, and the life."
John 14:6 nkjv

SATURDAY

A Hungry Heart Is Sharing

I love this old house. She's been in the family for close to half a century now. We, the current occupants, have gotten quite comfortable in her ample arms, and I love seeing the next generation napping in the bedroom Phil used as a boy or picking flowers in the same yard where he held neighborhood football games. On the other hand, the advancing age of our home means the grand dame has a few issues, especially where her plumbing is concerned. (I do hope you caught that. It was a great example of funny happening all by itself. If there's a trick to humor, it's mostly learning to pay attention, but we'll move on.)

Some home repairs one can afford to let slide. Water leaks do not fall in this category. Phil and I have learned from experience just how fast her trickles can turn into streams. God's Word compares this principle of water to a bone of contention in these wise words from Proverbs 17:14: "The beginning of strife is like letting out water, so abandon the quarrel before it breaks out." It's not necessary to have suffered a plumbing catastrophe to get that picture. Water and contention can be equally elusive if one isn't vigilant to restrain them, but there's another side to our analogy that's intriguing me at the moment.

The Good Book also uses water to symbolize the Word of God. As believers, we know that we are called to share the Good News with those around us, but have you considered that estimating our impact can also be elusive? We can spend our lives sharing Living Water with those around us without really knowing where it runs off and where it sinks in—that record belongs to the Father. There's a thirsty world around us, and you and I can spill out all over them. Let's do it today!

"He who believes in Me, as the Scripture said,
'From his innermost being will flow rivers of living water.'"

MONDAY

A Hungry Heart Is Surrendered

I've never had the opportunity to ride a bicycle built for two—but I've ridden double on many a bike meant for one. The experience might be similar, but I expect it's nowhere near as exciting. Riding double was our standard mode of transportation back on Bull Run Road. I'm talking about the extra seat, the one provided on the handlebars. If you've ever ridden up front, you know it can be exhilarating. Life is anything but dull when you're trying to balance on a tiny chrome bar while keeping your feet out of the spokes. Another plus to riding the handlebars is being able to benefit from someone else's labor. Neat.

Of course, there are times when riding up front can be less than pleasant. I remember several failed attempts at our rural version of tandem biking. Sometimes one of my visiting city boy cousins (who were almost always smaller and weaker than us girls) would decide he should be the one to peddle. Bad idea! Here's a handlebar lesson for the uninitiated: if the weaker one insists on peddling, the bike will wobble fitfully down the road at best and crash at worst. And it doesn't help if the weak one decides to stand up and put his pitiful might into it. The ride only gets shakier, making the experience even more uncomfortable for everyone involved.

I realize giving your life over to God can often feel as scary as riding on the handlebars, but it's a fantastic deal. Your Creator is fully capable of handling the job, and His offer is almost too good to believe. We can rest on the work His Son did on the cross by giving up and giving in. But that's where the rubber often hits the road, pun intended.

See, one of the things I remember about tandem biking is that along with putting the stronger one on the pedals, it is imperative that you not try and steer from the handlebars. Actually, it's outright dangerous! That's one time when two sets of hands never proved better than a single, skilled pair.

Sometimes we agree to ride on God's handlebars—as long as we still get to steer. Bad idea! God wants to power your trip and steer it, too. Are you scared? That's okay. It's even a bit healthy. Think of it as "hanging on for dear life" on the adventure of a lifetime.

"Call to Me, and I will answer you, and show you great and mighty things, which you do not know."
JEREMIAH 33:3 NKJV

TUESDAY

A Hungry Heart Is Intentional

I was fifteen when my parents built the brick home they still live in today. Those early building stages were exciting for all of us. I remember the day the foundation was poured and how my sisters and I felt duty bound to trace our names in the wet concrete beside the carport. Our artwork is frozen in time, much like the memory I have of my first look at the slab. Compared to the plans, the foundation seemed so much smaller than I had expected!

Over the years, I've learned that all foundations look smaller than their actual square footage, but my parents were clearly aware of this optical illusion at the time, for they were totally unfazed. They knew the foundation was only the first step in our new home; and since they weren't planning to throw sleeping bags down and set up house on that concrete rectangle, their focus was on the next stage. Construction went pretty much like they said it would after that. By the time the framework started going up and the walls started materializing, the house was much more like the dream home I had pictured.

I see a lesson tucked in that memory. To live this life without building on the foundation that is Jesus Christ is futile. Jesus said, "Everyone who hears these words of Mine and does not act on them, will be like a foolish man who built his house on the sand. The rain fell, and the floods came, and the winds blew and slammed against that house; and it fell—and great was its fall" (Matthew 7:26–27).

And yet to lay your foundation in Christ and stop there without working with Him to build the structure He wants your life to become—this is akin to living on cold, hard concrete. Anyone who does so is destined to be disappointed in the foundation. It's a tragedy that should never happen, but if it does, the fault is our own. All the building tools you and I will ever need are found between the pages of His living Word and in listening to His Spirit who comes to live in us. Let's seek His grace *and* His glory and discover the God who is more than we can hope for and greater than our dreams.

Now to Him who is able to do far more abundantly beyond
all that we ask or think, according to the power that works
within us, to Him be the glory in the church and in Christ
Jesus to all generations forever and ever. Amen.

Ephesians 3:20–21

WEDNESDAY

A Hungry Heart Is Praying

I was sitting on the back porch enjoying my morning devotion when my attention became arrested by a louder-than-usual mocking bird commotion on the far side of the oak tree. Curious, I decided to go see what the problem was, only Dixie Belle beat me to it. Much to my dismay, and her delight, we discovered that one of the curious babies had left the nest a little too early. Dixie immediately snatched the baby bird up and began to make a run for it, followed closely by a posse of angry mockingbirds, led by one irate ringleader who I suspected to be the mother of said bird and comprised of a number of her closest friends and relatives. I watched as those belligerent birds chased poor Dixie Belle all over the backyard in a well-choreographed attack. They took turns swooping, diving, and screeching at her head, but Dixie refused to hand the bird over.

After a while the mob, with the exception of the mama bird, lost interest and Dixie returned to show me her trophy. As you can imagine, I was less than impressed when she dropped her prize right in front of me and began to play with the injured appetizer. I tried to shame her into giving up the baby bird, but she just looked at me with a look that implied, "Say what you will. I am a bird dog. It's what I do."

Meanwhile, my heart was breaking as I watched that mama bird pacing and screeching within steps of the cruel scene. I was struck by the lesson playing out before me. What a picture of heartache! I know parents who feel as helpless as Mama Mockingbird. Their kids have an enemy whose very nature is to steal, kill, and destroy. He is aided by a culture that constantly beckons them to explore past the safety of their family structure and the parents who stand by fretting and wringing their hands. Your kids need to hear what you have to say and where you stand. By all means, talk to them—about everything—and do it often. However, I'd like to respectfully encourage you to forgo some of the pacing and screeching in favor of something infinitely more productive.

For here's the big difference between that grieving mama bird and believing parents. She may have been without recourse in the face of Dixie's attack, but you aren't! Pray, don't pace. Seek, don't screech. If you'll intercede, your God will intervene.

Be anxious for nothing, but in everything by prayer and supplication with thanksgiving let your requests be made known to God. And the peace of God, which surpasses all comprehension, will guard your hearts and your minds in Christ Jesus.

PHILIPPIANS 4:6–7

The more Christ is formed in us,
the more we become who
we're purposed to be.

❧ THURSDAY ❧

A Hungry Heart Is Celebrating

Years ago my best friend and I made a commitment to give the eulogy at each other's funeral. We felt confident that we both knew precisely the good-bye service the other one would want: a respectful but jubilant get-together with upbeat music, as much laughter as possible, and a heartfelt invitation for everyone present to trust the Jesus we live for and adore. The two of us felt good about our pact, until the day one of our brilliant friends pointed out that we couldn't actually speak at each other's funeral.

"And why not?" we asked in unison.

She answered in the tone one might use with a toddler, "Because somebody would have to come back from the grave to make the second one happen."

Oh. We were forced to agree that Mrs. Smarty Pants had a point. I suppose we could prepare our reciprocating eulogies in advance, but the idea doesn't appeal to either of us.

The media does that sort of thing all the time. Did you know that? They keep prepared obituaries for all kinds of famous people on file. They have obits ready for the aged and/or ill celebrity, and they have carefully crafted eulogies for the famous person who is publicly spinning out of control. Even if, chronologically speaking, the troubled star should have years to live, his or her obituary is often written and waiting for the date after the dash. Granted, someone still has to see that such an advance obit is updated and revised before it is published, lest it be filled with erroneous information. For there is only One who knows the end from the beginning.

That is good news for a ton of reasons, but here's one: our age-obsessed culture can make anyone over the age of twenty-five feel like yesterday's news, even if she or he is setting the world on fire! As we mature in years, we can be tempted to evaluate our lives based on the wrong perception of what a well-lived life looks like. The truth? Only God knows what we have been called to do in our years here on earth, and what we will do.

I'm freshly convinced that our struggle is not in unearthing and fulfilling this individual mission before our obituary is finalized. Rather, our challenge is to live with one main goal: to know God and celebrate the One whom He has sent, Jesus Christ, His Son. In doing this we can't help but become exactly who He purposed us to be.

Not that I have already obtained it or have already become perfect, but I press on so that I may lay hold of that for which also I was laid hold of by Christ Jesus.

PHILIPPIANS 3:12

FRIDAY

A Hungry Heart Is Needy

It was my own heavy sigh that startled me. Until that moment I wasn't fully aware that I was literally having an imaginary back-and-forth conversation with this other person. I was far too busy saying what I felt needed to be said. Someone needed to tell this person how the cow eats the cabbage, and I had apparently nominated myself for the job. Miss Thang needed to know how hurtful her words were.

Things had been going quite well in this imaginary conversation of mine, too—up until I heard myself sigh deeply at her response. That was quite the eye-opening moment. I was expressing my frustration over something the other person was saying, only I was the one writing her dialogue. Are you still with me?

Now, before anyone decides I should be medicated, let's have a little come-to-Jesus meeting. The truth is, I just say these things aloud, folks. We can all fall prey to playing out such scenarios. Take an inventory of your own thought life and see if I'm not telling it straight. The things that can happen in our head in a split second of time can be startling, at best.

It's why I tell Jesus on a regular basis that I need Him in all of my thoughts, because otherwise they have a blasted tendency of deteriorating. I've not always embraced this truth. I used to want "me time" in my own little head, separate from my devotional life. It wasn't that I wanted to think on ugly stuff. I just wanted quiet time for me with me. Thanks be to God, I now know that such isolation is a trap waiting to spring. Jesus has taught me that I need Him all day every day. And that's why anytime I realize that my thought life is crowding Jesus out, I invite Him right back in.

Please don't misunderstand. I'm not saying it's wrong to feel anger, sadness, grief, or any other painful emotion. Heavens, no. I'm just asking us all to remember that indulging such feelings to the exclusion of God is an emotional death spiral. Let's choose life and ask Jesus to help us recognize these moments!

For as he thinketh in his heart, so is he.
PROVERBS 23:7 KJV

SATURDAY

A Hungry Heart Is Sharing

As y'all know by now, I grew up last in a ragtag line of three little tomboys. We lived in the country, in a small brick house on a gravel road called Bull Run Road. It's fairly easy to get there from here, but you'll need good directions. Our community was called Alsatia, and it was too small to have its own post office. Instead, our mailing address read Transylvania, Louisiana, a larger community just up the road. (And no, to answer your question, there were no vampires there. Although, to be fair, my sisters and I did draw one another's blood on occasion.)

My family wasn't poor and we never went without a meal, but we didn't have a lot of extras, at least not compared to today's kids. And, to add insult to what my sisters and I considered a grave injury, what we did have Mama fully expected us girls to share. It was an unpopular edict that led to a bit of conflict on Bull Run Road. Had you asked us, we girls would have agreed that "share and share alike" only sounds nice in theory. We had also learned that it wasn't wise to go against Mama. It's just that when one finds oneself holding the last MoonPie in the house, one finds practicing the theory more difficult.

Those years on Bull Run Road left my sisters and me with a

truckload of fond memories and some enduring life lessons. For instance, I see an important truth hidden in that MoonPie story: it is a whole lot easier to share when you have an abundance of what the other person needs.

It's a simple observation that can have deeper meaning if you'll give it a little thought. For just as surely as Mama wanted us girls to share our childhood possessions with each other, our heavenly Father wants us to share our faith and His amazing love with those around us. If sharing our faith sounds too difficult, it could just be that we don't have enough to divide! Ouch! How about it? Are you running on empty? Is your faith cabinet bare? If so, that's a problem with an ever-available fix. The God of the Bible is waiting to shower us with His pressed-down, shaken-together, running-out-all-over love. If we'll surrender to His will with complete abandon, He will fill us up with more than enough love to "share and share alike."

*Even if I am being poured out like a drink offering
on the sacrifice and service coming from your faith,
I am glad and rejoice with all of you.*
PHILIPPIANS 2:17 NIV

MONDAY

A Hungry Heart Is Surrendered

"Crack!" *Wait a minute,* I thought to my ten-year-old self. *What was that? Surely it wasn't—*

"Crack!" *Uh-oh, that's exactly what it was!*

This wasn't good. It just so happened that my legs and arms were at that very moment wrapped tightly around the very tree limb that was threatening to break. Yes, indeed. This was clearly going to be a big deal. No sooner did that sobering realization register than the limb in question gave way and I began to fall. Mind you, this all happened many moons ago now, but to the best of my storyteller's memory, I fell for three hours and ten minutes and hit twenty-seven branches on my way down to the hard-packed delta dirt. Okay, perhaps it would be more accurate to say I fell eight or nine feet through a couple of branches, but the point is that it was scary, and the landing was painful.

To be sure, Papa had warned me that climbing trees was dangerous and limbs could break at any time without warning. No doubt I had responded to all those admonitions many times over with something like, "Yes, sir, I know."

From that day forward, however, I wouldn't just know it, I would acknowledge it. By that I mean that I did climb trees again, but I never again placed myself in such a precarious position by putting all my weight on one branch.

Proverbs 3:6 tells us to acknowledge the Lord in all our ways and He will make our paths straight. I'd just like to remind us all that knowing about God is light-years from actually acknowledging God.

According to Webster, to acknowledge means to recognize the existence of something (or Someone in our case), to accept responsibility for that knowledge, and to act on it—much like I did by altering my tree-climbing methods. It all raises a very good question. Do we simply know about God, or do we acknowledge God in all our ways, leaning not on our own understanding, so that He might direct our paths?

Do not be wise in your own estimation.
ROMANS 12:16 HCSB

A Hungry Heart Is Intentional

My friend Rhonda and I are accustomed to juggling several conversation balls simultaneously. (If you listen to *All Things Southern Live* on the radio, you may have heard me call her the Madness Czar or Red. The names all refer to the same dear friend.)

Rhonda and I usually keep a minimum of three or four subjects going simultaneously, all while utilizing a handy-dandy notepad that we've taken to keeping between us. It's a neat tool we developed many years ago that lets the person who has stopped to breathe jot down notes of other intended topics without missing a detail of the story that has the floor. Granted, this torrid conversational pace is mostly a female thing. I've met a few men who can hang with it, but most members of the male species would rather have sharp needles stuck in their eyeballs than be forced to participate in such a word fest. Can I have a witness?

As you can imagine, it's not easy to get Rhonda and me to hit pause either, which is why we're always amused by the EF Hutton moments my lovely GSP navigator, Carmen the Garmin, inspires whenever we take her on an outing to an unknown destination. Do y'all remember the EF Hutton commercials? They once ingrained themselves in our national consciousness with that catchy phrase, "When EF Hutton talks, people listen." Well, I had not had Carmen the Garmin long at all when Rhonda and I noticed that she was wielding some sort of EF Hutton power over us. Every time she broke her silence, Rhonda and I would both put our hands up as if to signal, "Shush—Carmen's speaking!" Indeed, Carmen hadn't been on board very long before she had totally won our trust in her ability to save us from making a wrong turn.

Oh, that we believers would give the Word of God such rapt attention! We know the Bible says that God is willing to direct our paths, and we know He is fully capable of saving us from a wrong turn. The challenge is learning to stop long enough to hear Him speak. And yet that type of guidance is available if only we train ourselves to listen. I've found that the more I immerse myself in God's written Word, the more I hear Him speak to my heart. Try it. Soon His voice will be so recognizable that you'll hear Him when you're approaching one of life's intersections, and you'll be able to make the right choice with confidence.

Your ears will hear a word behind you, "This is the way,
walk in it," whenever you turn to the right or to the left.

ISAIAH 30:21

A Hungry Heart Is Praying

I couldn't tell you how I found the first article if my life depended on it. Those Internet rabbit chases can definitely sneak up on a person. A belle can be looking up a recipe one minute and watching video of a water-skiing squirrel the next. Oh, don't act like you haven't done it. I may have been born at night, but it wasn't last night.

As I traveled this particular rabbit trail, my curious self was led from one website to the next. With each click, my eyes took in images of abandoned church buildings in big cities and small towns all across our planet. The more I surfed, the more somber I became. As sad as it was to see those glorious cathedrals standing tomb silent as plaster cracked and fell from their elaborately carved architecture, the sagging walls of country churches being pulled to their foundations by snaking vines caught in my heart every bit as much or more. Toward the end of my "research," I sat studying the broken-down pulpit where someone once read holy words, and I thought I might cry.

See, I don't know the stories behind all of those abandoned churches, but I can't help wondering about how and why the decision was made to close their doors. I wonder if the people left all at once or if they moved away slowly, maybe from wars, economic troubles, or natural disasters. Perhaps the crowds dwindled almost imperceptibly until it seemed easier to walk away than it did to maintain those sacred structures.

Friends, I see a stirring charge here for all of us, and I'm not talking about material sanctuaries anymore. The apostle Paul once asked, "Do you not know that your body is a temple of the Holy Spirit who is in you, whom you have from God, and that you are not your own?" (1 Corinthians 6:19).

Considering that we, as believers, house the very presence of God is a staggering thought but a glorious truth. And the holy voice that once woke us from the dead is continuing to call us to Him for life-giving relationship. To neglect to listen is the first step in abandoning the sanctuary.

Beware the incremental fade that threatens our temples.

"Blessed are those who hear the word of God and observe it."
LUKE 11:28

A Hungry Heart Is Celebrating

I stared at the huge stone on the shiny gold band and looked up at the giver of the grand gift. What in the world should I say? He was so sweet, but I knew we were far too young.

With as much sophistication as my then second-grade self could muster, I took a deep breath and explained to my on-again, off-again boyfriend that I couldn't wear the ring he won at the fair because of our ages. I remember telling him that I didn't deserve such a nice gift, and it wouldn't be right for me to accept it. Time has blurred the rest of the details. Herbie—he goes by Herb now—probably shrugged his shoulders and ran off to join the elementary football game before the recess bell rang, leaving my dramatic little self to ponder the impact of this moment on our complicated relationship.

Oh, yes, that's a true story, and I really did think we were having a made-for-television moment. Seriously, y'all, when I stop and think about it, I realize that I've been this kind of strange for a long time. But that's okay. Our doomed grade-school romance is a great jumping-off place for our present discussion.

The more I fall for this God of ours, the more I marvel at the priceless gift of eternal life He offers all who will believe in Jesus

Christ, His Son and our Savior. This is no bauble. It's treasure untold. God promises to come in the Spirit and live in these dusty frames of ours, to walk us through this life and into the next; and neither you nor I have ever done a single thing to deserve such extravagant love!

God's gift is one that not even yours truly can overdramatize. What we can do is revel in it, on bended knee.

My goal is that they may be encouraged in heart and united in love,
so that they may have the full riches of complete understanding,
in order that they may know the mystery of God, namely, Christ,
in whom are hidden all the treasures of wisdom and knowledge.

COLOSSIANS 2:2–3 NIV

A Hungry Heart Is Needy

By the time my daughter arrived with her husband and boys, it had been weeks since she'd dropped a huge ceramic dish on her right foot, nearly severing the tendon of her big toe, but the story she recounted was still fresh. The painful accident had led to an emergency room visit with then four-year-old Connor in tow. Connor, we were told, was quite put out the entire time because she inadvertently left his afternoon popcorn in the microwave when they fled for medical help. For shame. The ER trip included multiple stitches and shots to guard against infection from the raw chicken the pot was holding before it created the open wound on my daughter's digit. Bless her.

Over the course of her stay, Jessica was updating us on the big toe boo-boo—and clearly trying to put the best possible spin on it—when she reported that it was mostly fine, except she couldn't bend it and she was *not* going back to the doctor. Scar tissue. We unanimously agreed that it was scar tissue and the doctor would break it for her if she did go. We had also begun to offer suggestions on how we could help her break the stubborn tissue when Carey came to her sister-in-law's defense.

"Please, no," Carey said. "No DIY medical procedures this year, y'all."

Jessica Ann voted yes on that idea faster than quick. It's hard to blame her. Over the years, this family has used everything from drills to duct tape to fix what ails us. I don't recommend any of those methods. Just say no to do-it-yourself medical procedures.

And while we're on the subject, say no to do-it-yourself Christianity, too. Satan is a sneaky proponent of this form of stinky self-help religion. He encourages us to try and act straight, do good, or have the right attitude all under our own steam. It's a trap, y'all.

The truth is God gives empowering grace to the one who goes to Him for it and then goes back to Him for it repeatedly. He gives grace to those who know how needy they are for Him and who draw on Jesus to live like Jesus. Bottom line; say no to do-it-yourself medical procedures. And say a bigger, more emphatic no to do-it-yourself religion! As James would say, "He giveth more grace."

He gives all the more grace.
JAMES 4:6 ISV

Sharing our faith stories allows
the One who gave them space
to speak through them.

SATURDAY

A Hungry Heart Is Sharing

Greeting my grands after a separation of any length is a charmingly noisy affair. I love listening to the breathless retellings of where they've been, what they've seen, and what they've done. Like littles everywhere, my grandchildren's excitement has a tendency to outpace their words.

Their communication challenges are further complicated by their ongoing competition for the floor. The oldest two, Grant and Emerson, do their best to pull rank on Carlisle and Connor. And then there's Weston the Wonder Boy, who is generally bringing up the rear on his chubby little legs and repeating every word the others are saying with equal enthusiasm. Bless their excitable hearts.

Tell me, do you remember the biblical story of the women who found Jesus' empty tomb? The Bible says they ran to the disciples to report their findings, but like my grands, I'm thinking their excitement got the best of them, too. Why? Because scripture says the women sounded like people telling idle tales, which is a Greek idiom for people who seem delirious. I can see them now.

"We saw an angel! Jesus was gone! We saw his grave clothes. Wait, did we say there was an angel—there were actually two. One sat on a rock. We saw another one inside!"

Indeed, it must've been hard to describe what they had seen. But guess what? Peter and John ran to the tomb to see what they were talking about! That tells us the women got enough of their message across to make the men want to investigate their claims.

This is what all of us believers should aim to do: share our experience of encountering the truth of Jesus Christ and how He has changed our lives. We don't have to quote chapter and verse for our efforts to lead our listeners to investigate our claims for themselves.

Will practice make us perfect storytellers? Probably not. And that's okay. Our job is to share the promise and trust the result to the Holy Spirit of God who gave us our stories in the first place.

My mouth shall tell of Your righteousness and of Your
salvation all day long; for I do not know the sum of them.
PSALM 71:15

*Through surrender the knowledge
of Jesus in our heads becomes the
presence of Jesus in our hearts.*

MONDAY

A Hungry Heart Is Surrendered

Hand in hand we strolled, just me and my sweet thang, browsing store after store filled with everything one could dream of spending one's money on—except we didn't. Oh, we commented on this, and we admired that, but more than anything we simply enjoyed spending the last beautiful day of October with several thousand of our closest friends in the downtown shopping super land of Gatlinburg, Tennessee, without a to-do list or a deadline in sight.

As a general rule, neither of us is really good about that sort of *Que Sera, Sera* living. The idea of downtime always sounds appealing when we're working like mad, he on the farm and me at the laptop, but we usually find kicking back for any length of time a bit harder to do. Update: we got a lot better at it on that Tennessee getaway.

We spent the better part of a day strolling those streets, and we didn't even make it to the second row of shops, those behind Main Street without nearly as much foot traffic. It prompted Phil to muse aloud as we headed out of town, "Location, location, location."

I agreed. Those stores were mere yards from the hustling and bustling paying customers on the city's thoroughfare, but they may as well have been located miles away from the action.

As I considered their situation, I thought about our own. On the drive back to our cabin in the woods, my man and I discussed the distance that can exist between our heads and our hearts. Indeed, the old saying is true, location is everything. You and I can know everything the Bible teaches about Jesus the Man, but if Jesus the Savior isn't residing and reigning in our hearts, that knowledge is of no benefit to us on either side of heaven. We may as well have lived and died without ever hearing His name.

Location, location, location. Where is Jesus in our lives?

For if anyone is a hearer of the word and not a doer, he is
like a man who looks at his natural face in a mirror;
for once he has looked at himself and gone away, he has
immediately forgotten what kind of person he was.

JAMES 1:23–24

TUESDAY

A Hungry Heart Is Intentional

Some funny old laws remain on the books today. Did you know it was once illegal in Arkansas to walk a cow down Main Street after 1:00 p.m. on Sundays? I suppose one was to get one's cow walking done early. Even stranger is how many of our laws addressed the elephant problem. Who knew we ever had one? In California you could only walk your elephant down Main Street if it was on a leash. And in Florida you could tie your elephant to a parking meter, but you had to pay just like you would for a vehicle. Ah, but then Minnesota got serious with those crazy pachyderms. You couldn't park your elephant on Minnesota streets with or without paying the meter. So there!

Other states had different wildlife problems. In Louisiana you could not tie an alligator to a fire hydrant, and no gorilla was allowed in the backseat of any car in Massachusetts. But this next one could be my favorite. Georgia lawmakers once made it a crime for a chicken to cross the road. My guess is they got tired of trying to figure out the blame chickens' motives!

Men can truly make a lot of funny laws, but sadly, they can also make evil ones. America has had her share of bad laws, but all over the world people have made statutes that bring true grief to those who must keep them. That reality makes me appreciate God's laws even more. Psalm 19:8 says, "The precepts of the LORD are right, rejoicing the heart."

Oh, friends, God's laws are not only in perfect agreement, but great joy awaits those who embrace the empowering grace that is ours through Christ to obey them.

Blessed are You, O LORD; teach me Your statutes.
PSALM 119:12

A Hungry Heart Is Praying

Exercise is such a habit. Having fallen in and out of it over the years, I know falling out is much easier. And yet I'm still prone to convincing myself that I'm too busy to exercise on a particular day, and I'm just going to miss this one little day. Okay, two at the most. You know how this ends, right? Before I can say, "I need chocolate," the habit is officially broken and it takes a supreme effort to get my exercise groove reestablished. Right now I'm trying to get my Chuck Norris Total Gym worked back into the routine as exercise equipment, instead of using it as a handy-dandy bench for the suitcase that remains in the perpetual state of being packed or unpacked. Mr. Norris would not be pleased.

Over the years, my beloved hubby and I have acquired just about every piece of exercise equipment on the market, each taking a turn in the corner of our bedroom, most of them late-night sucker purchases from an infomercial. None proved to be the magic bullet we hoped it might become. We've often said our dream machine would grab us as we walk by, slap cuffs on our wrists, and restrain us until we met the daily minimum. Of course, we both know that even if someone made such a machine, we would quickly learn to walk just outside of its reach. Bottom line, pun intended, the best exercise equipment can only offer access to a healthy body, never a guarantee.

This morning I was trying to commit a scripture verse to memory when I stopped once again to consider the word *access*. I love the second chapter of Ephesians! It talks about the access we have to God through the sacrifice of Jesus Christ. It's a phenomenal promise, but the truth is it doesn't guarantee that you'll ever enjoy His sweet fellowship any more than a machine can guarantee that Phil and I will become physically fit.

I do hope you're not waiting for God to hog-tie you and drag you into His wonderful presence. You'll be waiting for eternity, literally.

He Came And Preached Peace To You Who Were Far Away, And Peace To Those Who Were Near; for through Him we both have our access in one Spirit to the Father.
Ephesians 2:17–18

A Hungry Heart Is Celebrating

Did y'all see the movie titled *Her* by any chance? I didn't, but according to the reviews and previews, *Her* is a romance with a unique twist. One of the lovebirds, the female lead, is actually a highly advanced computer operating system, the other a lonely man whose marriage has failed. The man falls in love with this disembodied female voice on his smartphone, and apparently the rest of the movie is a study of their relationship and whether it is real. It's not treated as a comedy. The filmmaker behind *Her* describes it as "an original love story that explores the evolving nature—and the risks—of intimacy in the modern world."

Again, I haven't seen this movie, and it may have been quite entertaining, but from where I sit, having a conversation about the love affair between a man and his computer operating system has more to say about the woeful disconnect plaguing our endlessly connected selves than any evolving "risk of intimacy."

I don't believe the perils of relationships in our modern world are any riskier than they were when we used our number 2 pencils and sent love notes to our first-grade crushes. I remember full well how my heart pounded so hard I thought it would jump out of my chest. (Don't be such a grown-up; admit it. You remember that feeling, too.)

See, the truth is that loving others will always leave us vulnerable and exposed on some level, and yet we were born with a God-given desire for intimacy. So what are we to do? That's the good news. The answer for our condition is simple, really, and it's as old as the human race.

The ultimate security for our needy little hearts is found in celebrating and reciprocating the love that God lavished on the whole wide world on the cross. When our lives are built on Love Himself, we're able to have healthy relationships with other flesh-and-blood persons. Anything less, my friends, and well, we might just find ourselves engaged to our computers.

We love, because He first loved us.
1 John 4:19

FRIDAY

A Hungry Heart Is Needy

I'm writing to you from my favorite spot on the back porch. I can see the little blue nylon tent from here. The wind is threatening to tote it to the lake right now, and I'm tempted to let it. I'm at odds with that silly tent. Its story has continued to unfold from the day I pulled it out of the carrier it came in.

I bought the tent for my grandchildren; and just as I thought, the group deemed it a super-duper playhouse. Setting it up was as easy as the package advertised. It popped right out of its handy-dandy pouch, setting off squeals of delight from the All Things Southern grand czars. Returning it to the carrying case? That's where the real fun began. According to the instructions, collapsing it is a one-two-three type of thing. It's almost comical to watch the beloved hubby and me try to wrangle it into submission. We remain stuck on illustration number two.

Here's something to think about. The Bible calls these flesh-and-blood homes that our spirits are in "tents," too; and when the Lord comes to live in us, we see the new covenant fulfillment of the Old Testament tent of meeting where God descended to meet with man. We're often slow to admit it, but once we unfold this wonderful gift of salvation, we can find ourselves as challenged with handling this tent of meeting as I am with that store-bought job I'm watching in my peripheral vision.

I may never be able to manhandle that blue nylon tent, but I've learned a crucial lesson about dwelling in this flesh-and-blood tent with the Almighty. I can't manhandle my own personal mess, and I'm not meant to try. The Word teaches that, as believers, we've become the temple of God, His sanctuary. That same Word says we're increasingly transformed into His image, not by our efforts, but by looking away from ourselves and training our eyes on Jesus. Infatuation precedes transformation. Forget self. Behold the Lamb.

The next day [John] saw Jesus coming to him and said,
"Behold, the Lamb of God who takes away the sin of the world!"

JOHN 1:29

A Hungry Heart Is Sharing

I've just spent a considerable amount of time trying to track down the source of a familiar quote. It was a valiant effort to give credit where credit is due, but after a hundred dozen Internet rabbit holes, I surrender. I'm going to attribute the following words to Mr. Anonymous who once said, "Love is a choice."

Brilliant, that Mr. Anonymous. No sooner did he make his wise observation than everybody and their mama started repeating it. I'm sure you've heard it as often as I have. It's built into books, songs, and sermons. Relationship seminars and marriage retreats repeat it like a mantra. We're told, "Falling in love is easy. Staying in love is a choice." Whether spouses, kids, neighbors, or mean-as-a-striped-snake relatives, Mr. Anonymous wants us to know that we can choose to love them.

This is a good reminder to keep in our pockets. Especially since it's possible to love someone to death one minute and wonder if we could get away with it the next. Amen? So, no, I'm not trying to refute this widely accepted understanding that love is a choice. However, I would like to add to it, because my experience has been that simply choosing to love isn't quite the neat little fix either. Not if I'm looking to Shellie to make it happen. Stay with me. For people called to share the love of God, this is important.

I've discovered that I can choose love all I want, but if I'm looking to my own human heart to see it through, I'll find that the well I'm drawing from is far too shallow. It would be cause for despair if it weren't for the Good News. Turning to Jesus and asking Him to love through me allows me to draw from His bottomless resource! To be clear, this requires that I bend my will to Jesus over whatever is testing my "love," but if I deny my own response to yield to His, I get to both choose love and have access to the resource I need to walk it out. Yeah, you can quote me on that.

"The most important [commandment]. . .is this: . . .
'Love the Lord your God with all your heart and with
all your soul and with all your mind and with all your
strength.' The second is this: 'Love your neighbor as yourself.'
There is no commandment greater than these."
MARK 12:29–31 NIV

A Hungry Heart Is Surrendered

My daughter-in-law instructed her two oldest kids to get in the car while she finished packing the vehicle for another of our daylong photo shoots. Weston, the youngest of the three, was balanced on her hip. Carey was doing the food photography for my story-telling cookbook, *Hungry Is a Mighty Fine Sauce*, and she did a fabulous job. You can see more of her work in the recipe insert we have included in this book, but stay here for a minute—we have a story at hand.

Little Weston and Carey were still inside when then six-year-old Emerson stormed into the room in dramatic fashion, fully distraught because her little sister, Carlisle Mae, was in the wrong seat and she wouldn't move! It's the girls' practice to take turns riding in the Suburban's middle seat with Weston instead of on the unpopular third row. Emerson wanted Carey to take her side of the argument, but Carey was determined to use it as a teaching moment.

Once Carey managed to get Emerson to take a deep breath and calm down, she reminded her oldest daughter to think about the scripture they'd been studying, the one about preferring one another. She tried impressing on Emerson that where they sat in the car wasn't worth fighting about, and she asked Emerson what she thought Jesus would think about the situation.

Emerson stood quietly, soaking her mother's points in and nodding her head in agreement. Once dismissed, Emerson left the room with a calm and purposeful stride. Carey felt confident they were on the same page—until Emerson returned, moments later, more upset than before.

With her hands placed on her little hips in total outrage, Emerson announced, "I told Carlisle everything you said, and she still wouldn't move!"

In her defense, after a follow-up chat with her mom, Emerson really was able to let the whole thing go with a great attitude, but my, oh my, is this not a teaching moment for us all? And so I ask myself, what lesson is it I'm wanting someone else to hear that I actually need to apply to my own life? I would encourage you to join me in this prayer: oh, Jesus, we surrender our own agendas. Give us ears to hear!

"He who has ears to hear, let him hear."
MATTHEW 11:15

TUESDAY

A Hungry Heart Is Intentional

Ten years old may sound a little young to be on probation, but such was the case that summer years ago on Bull Run Road. I had used up all the goodwill of my wardens (a.k.a. parents) and had been subsequently threatened with all sorts of serious repercussions if I didn't start taking better care of my eyeglasses. Threats were not empty where I came from, but before I paint too harsh a picture of my dear parents, I should admit that I'd already managed to break or lose more eyeglasses in a few short years of wear than most people own in a lifetime. Hence the laying down of the law. Unfortunately, for me, I also had the attention span of a gnat on caffeine.

I distinctly remember sitting down on the end of the bed and hearing the unmistakable crunch of breaking glass. That horrible sound was followed almost immediately by a second grating noise, and it was almost worse than the first. That would be the detestable crowing voice of my middle sister. "You're gonna be in trouble," Rhonda sang in a singsong voice, obviously delighted by the prospect. *No joke,* I thought to myself. If I had learned anything in my ten years of living on Bull Run Road, it was that money didn't grow on trees. My folks were big on that particular nature lesson.

Only a couple of days had passed since Mama had picked up my latest pair of repaired glasses from the optician. I can't explain why fine china at a hunting camp was safer than eyeglasses in my possession, but it had become a fact of life. "You make 'em, I break 'em" seemed to be my involuntary mantra.

On the other hand, Rhonda's announcement was as dependable as daybreak. My dear sister could always be counted on to point out trouble—once it was headed my way and could no longer be avoided. Thanks a lot, sis. A heads-up is what I needed then, and it's what you and I still need today. We all need advance warnings in life, directions to avoid trouble before it's too late. So, here's a gentle reminder: God's Word is full of heads-ups for daily living. I can so appreciate the way the Word calls Jesus a brother "born for adversity" (Proverbs 17:17). Unlike my siblings, He doesn't delight in our blunders; He lives to save our souls and keep our feet from falling. May we all be diligent to open the Word and let Him direct us on the front end.

Let me hear Your lovingkindness in the morning;
for I trust in You; teach me the way in which
I should walk; for to You I lift up my soul.
PSALM 143:8

*Jesus is equally willing to help us
long for Him and to fulfill
that longing.*

WEDNESDAY

A Hungry Heart Is Praying

Can we talk about the grass that's supposed to be greener? You know, the life you could live if you weren't bound to this one. The job you could enjoy if you weren't stuck in the one that pays your bills. At best, the whole idea of greener grass will keep you from living the life God has for you right where you are. At worst, the lure of greener grass will bring your world crashing down around you.

I once had a conversation about this very thing with a small group of married women. One of the women had fallen into the trap of thinking about a previous relationship. She admitted to spending a lot of her time daydreaming about this other man, who was also married now, and she confessed to wanting to contact him.

We talked her away from the ledge, so to speak. I remember telling her that the enemy of her soul—and her marriage—was incredibly sneaky. Chances are, I told her, he is using this very technique on the wife of your old boyfriend. That woman could very well be thinking of the man she gave up to get the one you're longing for!

It's a devilish irony.

Our shaky acquaintance knew she was on dangerous ground.

Thankfully, she recognized the danger and didn't act on her impulses. That season passed. Sadly, many people don't succeed in avoiding the green-grass trap, but there's an antidote.

Making God the object of our longings positions us to recognize the enemy's schemes for what they are. The prophet Isaiah said, "Therefore the LORD longs to be gracious to you, and therefore He waits on high to have compassion on you. For the LORD is a God of justice." That's good stuff, but I love the promise in the closing line, "How blessed are all those who long for Him" (Isaiah 30:18).

The Lord longs for us, friends. We're blessed when we long for Him. And get this beautiful truth, born of my personal experience. If you don't long for Him but you want to, make it a prayer. He'll answer that, too!

> *"I will give them a heart to know Me, for I am the LORD;*
> *and they will be My people, and I will be their God,*
> *for they will return to Me with their whole heart."*

JEREMIAH 24:7

THURSDAY

A Hungry Heart Is Celebrating

Ah, the interesting universe of Hollywood and the megarich. There are many things celebrities do, say, and wear that I find off-putting, to say the least. But there are other things about their world that strike me as strange or funny. Or both. For the sake of today's discussion, I'd like to explore their red-carpet moments and the odd habit they—and the reporters that are tripping all over them—have of describing the clothes they've chosen to wear for the big night.

"Who are you wearing?" a gushing reporter will ask.

And the poised and smiling star will answer, "Kors! I'm wearing Kors!" It's not unusual to hear someone exclaim, "She wears him well."

Being a word person, and a visual one at that, this causes me to picture the star wobbling down the carpet in her high-priced heels with said fashion designer physically draped around her body. Yes, I know. I'm a simple girl. More so than you realize. I had to google "top fashion designer to the stars" just now to insert a plausible name into my imaginary scene. True story.

Because this clothes thing has fascinated me for some time, and because I'm an easy laugh, I have a recurring joke I usually post during the Grammys or Oscars, or any other time when the entertainment industry is all into who someone is wearing.

"I'm wearing Levi," I'll post to social media. "And my man is wearing Carhartt. And you?"

My readers get me, so they're usually quick to play along, and I have a blast joking with them. But let's switch gears a moment to something that shouldn't be taken lightly by any of us. The Word of God says that believers have literally put on Jesus, that we each are clothed in Christ (Galatians 3:27). While the stars may celebrate the name of a mere mortal draped about their bodies, I'd like to celebrate the name we believers wear that is above all others: Jesus, sweet Jesus. One day every knee will bow to this name. May it be said that those of us who wear Him, wear Him well.

Put on the Lord Jesus Christ, and make no provision for the flesh in regard to its lusts.
ROMANS 13:14

FRIDAY

A Hungry Heart Is Needy

Carlisle Mae went Christmas shopping all by herself last year. That's not an easy thing to do when you're five, but Carlisle is good at thinking outside the box. Her daddy, my number one son, bore witness to watching her latest stroke of ingenuity a couple weeks before the big family gift exchange.

Phillip was busy in his office one afternoon when Carlisle wandered into the room with a basket on her arm.

"Don't look," she instructed her daddy. "I'm Christmas shopping, and it's a secret."

Once she had Phillip's promise, Carlisle began browsing the bookshelves that line the far wall of her daddy's office. Did Phillip peek? Of course he did. My son watched out of the corner of his eye as his little girl considered first one item and then another. She was intentional and focused, acting much like you and me perusing the aisles of our favorite gift shop. After considerable thought, Carlisle Mae finally settled on a deer figurine to add to her cart. For his part, Phillip acted as if he hadn't seen a thing.

Days later, my son recounted this story to me and we both grinned from ear to ear. Even now, I'm smiling as I share this tale with you, for I find truth here.

I don't know if you can see your reflection in this tale, but it's not difficult for me to see myself. Whether we're talking about our time, talents, praises, or finances, we deceive ourselves if we think there is a single thing we can offer our heavenly Father that He hasn't given us first. Beginning with the air in our lungs, anything we have belongs to Him and everything we need comes from Him.

And yet on loan as these gifts are, God accepts them from us with loving affection. In the words of one of my favorite worship songs, He's a "good, good Father."

Behold, what manner of love the Father hath bestowed
upon us, that we should be called the sons of God.
1 JOHN 3:1 KJV

SATURDAY

A Hungry Heart Is Sharing

I love finding baby selfies on my iPhone, images of plump little lips belonging to wee ones who've managed to turn a camera phone on themselves long enough to capture partial glimpses of their own sweet faces. Oh yes, those please! I have one of Weston the Wonder Boy from Easter 2015 stored on my phone right now that could melt butter—and I've saved similar images from Emerson, Grant, Carlisle, and Connor.

Grandkids aside, however, today I want to talk about the big-people pouty lips and smiling selfies streaming endlessly on our social media walls. Please know that I am not venturing into this topic lightly. Some of my most favorite people in all the world post selfies now and again, so this is me proceeding respectfully and very carefully.

Are we good? Okay, consider this. Somewhere around ninety-three million selfies are posted daily. The numbers differ with who's counting and what platforms are being included, and Lord have mercy on my soul, that's not even counting the belfies. (If you don't know what a belfie is, count your blessings and ignore the reference.) By anyone's accounting, that's a whole lot of duck lips. These days we can even buy selfie poles to help extend our cameras for better self-portraits. This all raises a question.

What in the world?

The occasional group shot snagged selfie style because everyone wants to be in the picture is one thing, as is the special-event selfie and the random selfie itself. I'm talking about the need to consistently and repetitively pose alone and share it with the world.

What are we to make of this?

If a picture is worth a thousand words, could it be we're looking at mankind's incessant need to be seen, noticed, and/or acknowledged? I think so. And yet the fullest, grandest life is found, not in being acknowledged, but in acknowledging and beholding Jesus, the meeting place between God and man.

As followers of this Jesus, we've been called to die to self, not to promote it, but my experience has been that self has a thousand lives. Amen? I don't claim to have all the answers, but I do have an idea. The next time we're tempted to broadcast our own face, let's stop and seek His. If ever something needed to go viral, we're looking at it.

#SeekHisFace could change the world.

> *When You said, "Seek My face," my heart said to You,*
> *"Your face, O LORD, I shall seek."*
> PSALM 27:8

Scripture Index

OLD TESTAMENT

Deuteronomy
29:29 175

Joshua
1:8 173
23:8 159

Psalms
5:3 142
14:2 123
19:8 245
19:14 138
27:8 266
31:14 95
43:3 153
46:10 142
62:5 87
71:15 240
86:10 157
90:14 26
95:6 210
100:3 60
116:1 38
118:24 .106
119:12 .245
126:5–6 .52
139:13–18 45
139:16 .155
143:8 257
147:10–11 145

Proverbs
3:6 229
4:25–26 206
8:32 192
14:12 147
16:2 147
17:14 213
17:17 257
23:7 . . . . 134, 225
24:13–14 40
30:5 23

Isaiah
30:18 260
30:21 231
40:28 130
40:31 194
41:17 167
55:1 . . . . .6, 81
62:5 93

Jeremiah
24:7 260
33:3 . . . . 64, 216

Lamentations
3:26...................169

Hosea
6:3....................125
14:2...................104

NEW
TESTAMENT

Matthew
4:4....................114
5:16............... 19, 84
6:7.....................77
6:33...................203
7:7.....................91
7:26–27................218
11:15..................255
11:16–17................99
16:25............. 21, 190

Mark
4:34....................91
12:29–31...............253

Luke
11:28..................233
12:20–21...............110
18:1...................194

John
1:16............. 186, 208
1:29...................251
1:42....................67
3:16...................184

3:30...................162
6:63....................36
7:37–38.................30
7:38...................214
10:3...................169
10:27..................191
12:24....................9
14:6...................212
14:26..................128
15:5............... 34, 56
15:9...................118
17:25–26...............159
20:27..................132

Acts
1:8....................188
17:11...................11
17:26–28................15

Romans
5:8.....................28
5:10....................28
6:14....................69
8:29...................201
12:16..................229
13:14..................262

1 Corinthians
3:2.....................89
6:19...................233
15:31...................47

2 Corinthians
1:21–22.................54
3:2....................165

3:18 . . . . 43, 157
3:18-20 201
4:7 58
5:19 71
9:15 171
13:14 179

Galatians
3:27 262
6:10 149

Ephesians
1:3 185
1:6 99
2:13 136
2:17–18 247
3:17–19 140
3:20–21 218
4:15 13
4:32 32
5:8 79

Philippians
1:6 177
2:17 227
3:8 108
3:12 223
4:6–7 220
4:7 199

Colossians
1:10–12 112
2:2–3 235

1 Thessalonians
5:17 38

2 Timothy
2:15 128
3:16–17 175

Philemon
1:6 162

Hebrews
4:12 62
4:16 182
8:12 196
12:28–29 101
12:29 73
13:8 75

James
1:5 50
1:14–15 17
1:23–24 243
4:6 237
4:8 151
4:14 110
5:13 116

1 Peter
3:15 97

1 John
1:7 79
3:1 . . . . 67, 264
4:19 249
5:4 121
5:5 120
5:12 206

Revelation
5:8 155
19:15 62
22:17 93

About the Author

Shellie Rushing Tomlinson is a Jesus-loving, humor-gathering author, speaker, radio host, and down-home southern cook who believes the best meals come with a story. She and her farming husband live in Louisiana. They have two happily married children and five grandchildren.